Elisha

The Man of God

Hamilton Smith

Scripture Truth Publications

ELISHA

Hardback edition first published 1932 by The Central Bible Truth Depot, London

Transferred to Digital Printing 2007

ISBN: 978-0-901860-79-8 (paperback)

© Copyright 1932 The Central Bible Truth Depot and 2007 Scripture Truth

A publication of Scripture Truth

All rights reserved. No part of this publication may be reproduced, stored in a retrieval system, or transmitted, in any form or by any means, electronic, mechanical, photocopying, recording or otherwise without prior permission of Scripture Truth Publications.

Scripture quotations, unless otherwise indicated, are taken from The Authorized (King James) Version. Rights in the Authorized Version are vested in the Crown. Reproduced by permission of the Crown's patentee, Cambridge University Press.

Scripture quotations marked "N.Tr." are taken from "The Holy Scriptures, a New Translation from the Original Languages" by J. N. Darby (G Morrish, 1890)

Cover photograph ©iStockphoto.com/iacon (Jeffery Borchert)

Published by Scripture Truth Publications
Coopies Way, Coopies Lane,
Morpeth, Northumberland, NE61 6JN

Scripture Truth is an imprint of Central Bible Hammond Trust, a charitable trust

Typesetting by John Rice
Printed and bound by Lightning Source

Preface

The meaning of the name Elisha is "God the Saviour"; and, in conformity with his name, he was used, above all prophets in Old Testament days, to set forth the sovereign grace and mercy of God to a guilty people. In his day the Rulers, and institutions of the land in the hands of the Priesthood, had entirely failed to maintain the people in relationship with God. The warnings of Elijah had failed to recall the people to God. Thus, the utter ruin of God's people being manifested, God falls back upon His own sovereignty and raises up a man who, independent of the sacred and divinely appointed temple, and the official and divinely appointed Priesthood, goes through the Land of the apostate ten tribes performing miracles of mercy, and dispensing the grace of God to all who have faith to avail themselves of it.

Thus, in the history of Elisha, we see an illustration of the important principle that though God appoints institutions for His people to observe, He is not bound by them, nor limited to them, if man fails in his responsibility. In all these ways of sovereign grace Elisha has the high honour of foreshadowing the coming of Christ, the Anointed of God, who, in His day, went about doing good, apart from the authority of Priests and Rulers, asserting the sovereign right of God to rise above the institutions of the law, such as the Sabbath, in order to show grace to sinners.

ELISHA

ELISHA

Contents

1. Introduction 7
2. The Call of Elisha *1 Kings 19:14-21* 11
3. The Servant's Training *2 Kings 2:1-14* 14
4. The Sons of the Prophets *2 Kings 2:15-18* 23
5. The Men of the City *2 Kings 2:19-22* 26
6. The Mockers of Bethel *2 Kings 2:23-25* 28
7. The Kings and Their Armies *2 Kings 3* 30
8. The Widow's Oil *2 Kings 4:1-7* 35
9. The Shunammite *2 Kings 4:8-37*. 39
10. The Time of Dearth *2 Kings 4:38-41* 46
11. The Multitude Fed *2 Kings 4:42-44* 50
12. The Healing of the Leper *2 Kings 5:1-19* 52
13. The Servant of the Prophet *2 Kings 5:20-27* 61
14. The Borrowed Axe *2 Kings 6:1-7* 64
15. The Syrian Raids *2 Kings 6:8-23* 66
16. The Siege of Samaria *2 Kings 6:24-7:20* 70
17. The Seven Years' Famine *2 Kings 8:1-6* 77
18. The King of Syria *2 Kings 8:7-15* 80
19. The Anointing of Jehu *2 Kings 9* 84
20. The Death of Elisha *2 Kings 13:14-25* 86

ELISHA

1. Introduction

Never, in the course of Israel's history, had the moral condition of the nation been so low as in the reign of king Ahab. Of this weak and wicked man we read, that he "did evil in the sight of the Lord above all that were before him." The law was broken. The worship of idols was all but universal: men bowed down to the golden calves at Bethel and Dan: false prophets conducted their idolatrous rites in Jehovah's land. Under the leadership of the king, and his idolatrous wife, the nation had apostatized from Jehovah, and proved itself ripe for judgment.

Nevertheless, God lingers over this judgment-doomed nation. Instead of overwhelming the people with the judgment they deserve, God sends His prophet Elijah to expose their true condition and recall them to Himself. The life and miracles of Elijah had been one long witness against the nation's utter apostasy from the moral law and the worship of Jehovah. The years of drought, the fire from heaven, the destruction of the prophets of Baal, the judgment of the Captains and their Fifties, the doom pronounced against the king in the vineyard of Naboth, and the letter to the apostate king of Judah, foretelling a coming plague, were all solemn denunciations of prevailing evils.

Alas! the ministry of Elijah only brought to light the utter ruin of the nation in responsibility. It clearly showed that, not only the nation had broken the law, and sunk into idolatry, but that prophecy—which recalls a failing people to God—was entirely powerless to effect any restoration. In spite of a ministry accompanied by the warning signs of a famine on earth, and fire from heaven, the prophet of God is rejected by a blinded and idolatrous nation. Having fulfilled his ministry, the faithful but rejected prophet forsakes the land of Israel by way of Jordan—the river of death—and is taken to heaven by the whirlwind.

Thus as far as Israel is concerned, all is over. The nation has utterly failed to secure, or maintain, the blessing of God on the ground of the fulfilment of its responsibilities. Apparently nothing remains but the execution of the judgment they deserve. Here, however, we are permitted to see the wonders of the ways of God. For God uses the wickedness of man to disclose the resources of His own heart. Man had utterly failed, and God had shewn that He is not indifferent to sin, and in His own time must act in judgment. Nevertheless, God is sovereign, and reserves to Himself His sovereign rights of grace. Thus it comes to pass, that instead of cutting off the nation in judgment, God falls back on His sovereign grace. On the one hand He secures for Himself a remnant that have not bowed the knee to Baal; on the other hand He sends to a guilty nation a ministry of grace for every one who has faith to avail himself of grace. This ministry, being a ministry of grace, cannot be confined to the bounds of Israel. Its source lies outside the land, and, while sent to Israel, is available to the Gentile.

Elisha is the chosen vessel to carry this new ministry of grace to a ruined world. As one has said Elisha "completes by a ministry of grace in the power of life, what Elijah had begun in righteousness against idolatry." Elisha returns to

INTRODUCTION

the land that Elijah had left. The curse was there; widows are in need; hunger and famine are in the land; enemies oppose and death is over all. Into this scene of sin and ruin Elisha comes with power from on high, to display, in the midst of a dark world, the grace of heaven that can meet the need of man. Thus it comes to pass as Elisha passes on his way, the curse is removed; the needs of the widow are met; the barren woman becomes fruitful; the dead are raised; evil is averted; the hungry are fed; the leper is healed; enemies are baffled and defeated; earth's famine yields before heaven's plenty, and out of death there comes forth life.

Thus it becomes manifest that the ministry of Elisha wears an entirely different character to that of his great forerunner. Moreover, the manner of life of the two prophets, while in keeping with their respective ministries, was of necessity wholly different. Elijah led a life, for the most part, remote from the haunts of men: Elisha moved among the masses, on familiar terms with his fellow-men. Elijah was found by lonely streams, in desert ways and mountain caves: Elisha is found in the cities of men, and the camps of kings. Elijah is entertained by a humble widow of Sarepta: Elisha is the guest of the rich woman of Shunem.

These differences of life and manners were right and beautiful in their season. It was fitting that the one who has been rightly described as "the sworn enemy of all persons and institutions which interfered with the honour of the Lord God of Israel", should lead a life of strict separation from the nation that he so sternly condemned. Equally right that the one whose great mission is to declare the mercy of God to a guilty world, should freely move amongst his fellow men.

Nevertheless, the prophets were alike in their holy separation from the evils of the times. If Elisha moves amongst his fellow men as the intimate of kings and, at times, the companion of the great of the earth, he is wholly apart from the evil of their lives. He brings mercy to the guilty but walks apart from their guilt. He enriches others with the blessings of heaven, though content to remain a poor man on earth. As another has so truly said, "It was for others he occupied his resources and strength in God. He was rich, but not for himself… Thus—he meets the inconveniences of nature;—without a purse he relieves the poor;—without a commissariat he feeds armies;—the deadly thing he makes harmless;—without bread he gives food to a multitude, and gathers fragments;—without medicine he heals disease;—without armies or soldiers, he defeats enemies;—in famine he supplies a nation;—though dead he communicates life."

May we not add that, in all these shining ways of grace, Elisha is leading our thoughts to that far greater One who became poor that we through His poverty might be rich. In the spirit of Elijah, the great forerunner of Christ had dwelt in desert places, there to bring to light a godly remnant, and there to denounce the evils of a wicked and adulterous generation. Thus he prepared the way of the Lord, who, as the Son of Man, came "eating and drinking" with the children of men, as He moved amongst the needy crowds, dispensing the grace of God in a ruined world.

2. The Call of Elisha

1 KINGS 19:14-21

Elisha is first brought to our notice in the Lord's charge to Elijah, in the day of the prophet's despondency. Disappointed at the failure of his mission, embittered against the professing people of God, and occupied with himself, Elijah had, with a wounded spirit, spoken well of himself and nothing but evil of God's people. He imagined that he alone was standing for God, and that the entire nation was against him, seeking his life to take it away.

Elijah has to learn that the Lord has other instruments to carry out His government; other servants to maintain a witness for Himself; and, amongst the people of God, seven thousand that have not bowed the knee to Baal. Thus it comes to pass that Elijah has to retrace his steps from Horeb and anoint Elisha, the son of Shaphat, as prophet in his room.

How often in our own day, with its increasing corruption, we, with our limited outlook, may be led to imagine that the work of God depends upon one or two devoted and faithful servants of the Lord, and that with their removal all testimony for the Lord will cease. We have to learn that though servants pass God remains, and that God has other servants in preparation for His service, and, unknown to us, God has His hidden ones who have not bowed down to prevailing evils.

In obedience to the Lord's word, Elijah departs from Horeb to seek Elisha. The one chosen to take the place of the prophet is not found amongst the great men of the earth. God is no respecter of persons, and in choosing His servants God is not restricted to the great and noble. He may indeed employ the rich and the learned, kings and priests, as He sees fit. But at times He pours contempt on all our pride by taking up a man from the humblest walks of life to perform the highest spiritual service. He can use a little maid to bless a great man; He can take a lad from the sheepfolds to be the leader of His people Israel; He can use the betrothed of a carpenter to bring into this scene the Saviour of the world; and having brought the Saviour into the world, He can use some lowly fishermen to turn the world upside down. Thus it comes to pass, in the days of Elijah, He calls a simple husbandman from following the plough to be the prophet of his age.

Moreover, those that God calls to His service, are not the idle and ease-loving men of the world. Elisha is patiently pursuing his calling "ploughing with twelve yoke of oxen before him, and he with the twelfth", when the call comes. So David, in an earlier day, was keeping the sheep when called to be the king. And the disciples of a later day were casting their nets into the sea, or mending nets, when called to follow the King of kings.

It is upon this busy man that Elijah casts his mantle, an act that may signify that Elisha is called to take the place, exhibit the character, and act in the spirit of its owner. And thus the spiritual instincts of Elisha would appear to interpret the act, for we read, "He left the oxen and ran after

THE CALL OF ELISHA

Elijah." If, however, there is a divinely given readiness to follow Elijah, there is a natural reluctance to leave his loved ones. So he can say, "Let, me, I pray thee, kiss my father and my mother, and then I will follow thee." Elijah's answer throws the responsibility of responding to God's call entirely upon Elisha. "Go back again," he says, "for what have I done to thee?" He will use neither force nor command. No pressure shall be put on Elisha: he is left to discern the import of Elijah's action, and he is free to "go back" to his loved ones, or go forward with the rejected and persecuted prophet.

If Elisha's actions betray some looking back to the things that are behind, they also prove him to be an overcomer that celebrates his surrender of his things by providing a feast for others. In his day and measure, as one has remarked, he sold what he had and gave to the poor. Having thus finished with his earthly calling, "he arose, and went after Elijah, and ministered unto him." The man that had hitherto patiently pursued the daily round, toiling in the field, is now to be prepared to set forth the wonders of God's grace by following Elijah as his servant and companion.

3. The Servant's Training
2 KINGS 2:1-14

We hear nothing of Elisha from the time of his call, until the day when Elijah is translated. This we can understand, seeing that Elisha was anointed to be the prophet in the room of Elijah. The two ministries could not co-exist. When, however, the end of Elijah's pilgrimage is reached, Elisha comes to the front as the companion of his last journey and the witness of his rapture. As we follow these men of God in these mystic scenes, does it not become clear that the circumstances connected with Elijah's translation to heaven, become Elisha's preparation for service on earth?

How often we are permitted to see, in Scripture, that God trains in secret those whom He purposes to use in public. Joseph has his secret training with God in prison, before he can be a public witness for God in the palace. For forty years Moses keeps the flock of Jethro at the back of the desert, before he becomes the leader of God's flock through the desert. Unknown to others, David overcomes the lion and the bear, before he publicly enters into conflict with the giant. So Elisha must have his training as the servant and companion of Elijah, before he can take his place as the prophet of God and the witness of grace. Thus only will he be a vessel meet and fit for the Master's use and prepared unto every good work.

In this last journey there are scenes to be visited, tests to be faced, and lessons to be learnt. The places visited, so famous in Israel's history with God, must surely have had deep significance for Elisha as indeed for all who would serve the Lord.

Gilgal, the starting point of their journey, was the place of Israel's first encampment in the land, after their passage of the Jordan. There the people were circumcised, and there the Lord could say to Joshua, "This day have I rolled away the reproach of Egypt from off you" (Joshua 4:19; 5:2-9). In the light of Christianity we are privileged to enter into the spiritual meaning of circumcision. From the Epistle to the Colossians we understand that this rite sets forth the judgment of the body of the flesh in the death of Christ, and the believer's practical mortification of the flesh (Colossians 2:11; 3:5). Not only has God dealt with the believer's sins, but, at the cross, God has dealt with the old man that produced the sins. God's abhorrence of the flesh, His judgment upon the flesh, and His sentence of death against the flesh, have all been expressed in, and borne by, Christ on the cross. So the believer can say, "Our old man has been crucified with Christ." On the ground of what God has wrought through Christ, the believer is exhorted to "mortify" every form in which the flesh may seek to show itself. We are to treat every expression of the flesh as a member of that "old man" upon which death has been executed. If the flesh is thus judged the reproach of Egypt will be rolled away from us. It will no longer be manifest that we have ever been in the world; the manner of life we lived when in the world will no longer be allowed or seen. How deeply important that we should learn, and put in practice, this first great lesson, if we, in our day, are to be, in any sense, in the room of the glorious Man that has gone to heaven.

Bethel was the second stage of the journey—a place famous in the history of the patriarch Jacob (Genesis 28:15-19). There the Lord appeared to poor failing Jacob in the dreary place where his sin had cast him, and in sovereign grace blessed him unconditionally. For twenty years Jacob was to be a wanderer in strange lands; but he is assured that God will be with him, God will keep him, God will bring him again to the Land, and that God will be true to His word. Thus Elisha, at the commencement of his ministry, is assured, like Jacob of old, that he is blessed by the sovereign grace of a faithful God of which he is to become the witness. Good too if we take our pilgrim journey in all the blessed assurance that God is with us, will support us, and bring us at last to see for ourselves that what His love has purposed for us is the only thing worth living for.

Jericho is the next halting place in this remarkable journey. It was by Jericho that Joshua had the revelation of the Captain of the host of the Lord, with the drawn sword. At Jericho, too, the people first encountered the enemy that barred their entrance to the Land; there to learn that the Captain of the Lord's host was mightier than all the power of the enemy (Joshua 5:13-15; 6). Good for the man who is going to witness before kings and face their murderous hatred, to be reminded that in fighting the Lord's battles he will be supported by the Lord's host directed by the Captain of the host. And so, in after years, Elisha found, when besieged in Dothan by a host with horses and chariots, that the power for him was greater than the host of the Syrians that encompassed him, for "Behold, the mountain was full of horses and chariots of fire." In this the Christian day, it is still our privilege to take our journey to glory, and face every enemy, that disputes our present possession and enjoyment of God's purpose for us, under the leadership of the Captain of our salvation (Hebrews 2:10).

The last stage of this notable journey is reached at Jordan, the river that is such a constant type of actual death by which all links with the world are broken. Both Elijah and Elisha cross it, indeed, dry shod; but typically they pass through death, one to ascend to heavenly scenes, the other to witness of heavenly grace in a world to which in spirit he is dead.

Thus, may we not say, that through these notable places, Elisha is reminded, and we are to learn, at Gilgal *the holiness of God* that demands the judgment of the flesh; at Bethel *the unchanging grace of God* which blesses us, keeps us, and secures to us the end of our journey; at Jericho *the mighty power of God* by which we are sustained; and at Jordan, of *separation from the world* that we may enter upon heavenly ground and become the witnesses of a heavenly life that, setting forth the grace of God, can say, "Is it a time to receive money, and to receive garments, and oliveyards, and vineyards, and sheep, and oxen, and menservants, and maidservants?" (2 Kings 5:26).

Furthermore, not only is Elisha reminded of great truths at the different stages of this last journey, but his affections are put to the test by Elijah's thrice repeated words, "Tarry here, I pray thee." The instructions to go forward to these different places were given to Elijah. No command was given to Elisha to accompany him. If then he follows Elijah it is wholly a question of affection. And the test draws out his affection, for three times Elisha replies, "As the Lord liveth, and as thy soul liveth, *I will not leave thee.*"

Has this no voice for believers in this our day? Is it not by affection for Christ that we are moved to learn the lessons that come before us in the different stages of this striking journey? The doctrine of God's judgment on the flesh, must first be learned as the starting point of our identification with Christ; for who can walk with Christ with unjudged flesh? But can it be learnt otherwise than by hearts that are set upon Christ? Then, too, the truth of the House of God, set forth by Bethel, discovering to us the purpose of God, can only be learnt by a heart that longs to know the mind of Christ. Further, God's judgment on the world system, set forth in Jericho, can only be entered into by one, who in mind and affection is set upon another world. Lastly, the lesson of Jordan—the waiving and setting aside of the earthly order in favour of a present heavenly order of things, calls for a love that can overcome the land that flows with milk and honey, by being set upon the Man that has gone to heaven.

Moreover, there were those who twice reminded Elisha that the Lord was about to take away his master. These sons of the prophets, with more knowledge than heart, would only hinder Elisha's communion with his master, by occupying him with himself and his loss. Elisha silences these intrusions upon his soul's communion by saying, "I know it; hold ye your peace." He says, as it were, "Why should I not go with my lord Elijah and learn what it means to be *in his company* at Gilgal? Why should I not learn *with him* the lesson of Bethel? Why should I be parted *from him,* when passing through Jericho? Why should I not be *identified with him* in his passage through Jordan, even if it means leaving behind the earthly blessings of the Land, to be found with him in the outside place of reproach; for beyond the place of reproach there is another scene, a heavenly scene, and my affections are captured by the one that is going into that new scene?"

Thus the last stage of the journey is reached. Intruders have been silenced, affections have been kindled, leading Elisha

THE SERVANT'S TRAINING

to cleave to his master through all these changing scenes. The parting moment has come; Elijah is about to be rapt to heaven; Elisha, bereft of his master, is to be left behind in an apostatizing religious nation, who once were Jehovah's people. In this solemn moment Elijah utters his final word, "Ask what I shall do for thee, before I be taken away from thee." Could this offer have been made before? Is it not, as it were, the supreme test for Elisha? Will not the answer make manifest whether Elisha has entered into the spirit of his call? Whether he has profited by his companionship with Elijah? Whether, above all, he has learnt the lessons of Gilgal, Bethel, Jericho, and Jordan? Will it not make manifest whether Elisha has before him earthly gain, fleshly ambition, and worldly power, or is his sole purpose henceforth to be in the prophet's room, and witness to the sovereign grace of God as the representative of man that has gone to heaven?

Very blessedly Elisha's answer discloses his single-hearted devotedness. He asks for neither long life, nor earthly riches, nor worldly fame. He covets none of those things the natural man values, but rather that which the spiritual man needs; for he says, "Let a double portion of thy spirit be upon me." This by no means implies that he asks for twice as much gift, or power, as Elijah possessed. The Hebrew word implies the double portion of the elder son (Deuteronomy 21:17). Only Elisha asks not for a double portion of material wealth, but for a double portion of spiritual power. Other prophets will need spiritual power, but, if Elisha is anointed to take the place of Elijah—to be in his room—then, indeed, he will require a spiritual power twice as much as that of any other prophet.

Elijah replies, "Thou hast asked a hard thing." To gain riches, and fame, and worldly power, may entail toil and vexation of spirit, but they are not "hard" things, for men of the world can obtain these material advantages. To obtain, or confer, spiritual power is entirely outside the capabilities of the natural man. Nevertheless, says Elijah, "If thou see me when I am taken from thee, it shall be so unto thee; but if not it shall not be so." The granting of his request for a double portion of spiritual power, is made to turn upon Elisha seeing Elijah in his new position as the ascended man. The sight of Elijah in heaven will be the secret of Elisha's power on earth.

Herein, surely, are mysteries of which Christianity has revealed the spiritual meaning. For do we not know that faith's vision of Christ in the glory is the secret of power for the Christian on earth? Was it not strikingly so in the case of the first Christian martyr, for looking up steadfastly into heaven he could say, "Behold, I see the heavens opened, and the Son of Man standing on the right hand of God." In the light of that vision Stephen was so endued with power from on high that, like his Master, he can pray for his murderers, and, amidst the falling stones, calmly commit his spirit to the Lord Jesus. So, too, the Apostle of the Gentiles, commences his Christian career with the sight of Christ in the glory; and in the light of that vision he walked as a witness for Christ on earth through all the years of his devoted life. For ourselves does not the same Apostle tell us that, "We all looking on the glory of the Lord with unveiled face are transformed according to the same image from glory to glory" (2 Corinthians 3:18, N.Tr.)? We must catch the vision of the Lord in glory, if in any sense we are to represent on earth that blessed and perfect Man who has gone to glory.

So it came to pass, "as they still went on and talked, that, behold there appeared a chariot of fire, and horses of fire, and parted them both asunder; and Elijah went up by a whirlwind into heaven." Elisha saw it, and cried, "My father, my father, the chariot of Israel and the horsemen thereof."

Nothing quite like this great scene had ever taken place on earth. As one has said, "It is far above the silent removal of Enoch, and far below the calm majesty, of the ascension, when no chariots of fire were needed to sweep the Risen Body of the Redeemer from the earth: when as they beheld, He was taken up, and a cloud received Him out of their sight."

If, however, Elisha sees his master ascend to heaven, we also read, "He saw him no more." He sees him in the heavens to which he had ascended, but on earth he sees him no more. Has this no voice for the Christian? Does not the Apostle say, "Henceforth know we no man after the flesh: yea, though we have known Christ after the flesh, yet now henceforth know we Him no more" (2 Corinthians 5:16)? Words that by no means imply that we are not to consider Christ in His path through this world, and learn of Him, as we delight our souls in His lowly grace, His tender love, and infinite holiness. They plainly tell us, however, that we are no longer to know Him in connection with Israel and this world. We are, rather, to know Him as the Leader of a heavenly band, and in heavenly relationships. Devoted but ignorant disciples, may say, "We trusted that it had been He which should have redeemed Israel." Corrupt Christendom may attempt to connect the Name of Christ with their schemes for the improvement of man and the betterment of the world; but the Christian taught in the mind of the Lord will take his place outside the world, while pressing on to Christ in glory, refusing to connect Christ with a world that nailed Him to the cross.

The result of thus knowing Christ in His new place in heaven is very happily set forth in picture in the case of

Elisha. The vision of the ascended Elijah leads to a twofold action on his part. First "he took hold of his own clothes, and rent them in pieces"; an act that signifies the laying aside of one character in order to exhibit a character that is entirely new, for the garment speaks of the practical righteousness of the saints and the character they exhibit before the world. Elisha did not simply lay them aside to be taken again on certain occasions; he made them useless for future wear by rending them in twain. Then, secondly, "He took up also the mantle of Elijah that fell from him." Henceforth he will exhibit the character of the man that has gone to heaven. So, too, the Apostle after saying we know Christ no more after the flesh, can go on to say, "Therefore if any man be in Christ, he is a new creature: old things are passed away: behold, all things are become new."

At once Elisha acts in the power of the new life. He comes back into a ruined nation, guilty of having broken the law, defiled by idolatry, and apostate from Jehovah, and in the midst of this scene of wretchedness and desolation he presents the sovereignty of God rising above all man's sin, and acting in the supremacy of grace for those who have faith to avail themselves of blessing on the ground of grace.

4. The Sons of the Prophets
2 KINGS 2:15-18

The blessed effects of Elisha's training are now made manifest to others. He becomes a witness before the world of the one that has gone to heaven. The sons of the prophets take note of his new character; for, looking upon Elisha, they say, "The spirit of Elijah doth rest upon Elisha." They look at a man on earth, and they see the spirit and character of a man in heaven.

Has this no voice for us in this Christian day? Does this not set forth in picture our highest privilege and responsibility as Christians? For are we not left on earth to represent the Man in the glory? Paul could speak of the Corinthian saints as being "Christ's epistle" known and read of all men. The Spirit had written Christ in their hearts, and, in the measure in which the Spirit read Christ in their hearts, the world read Christ in their lives.

Alas! are we not too often like the sons of the prophets, who could appreciate the spirit of Elijah in another, though exhibiting little of this spirit in themselves? They had a measure of knowledge, for they knew when the moment had come for Elijah to be rapt to heaven, but they had no heart to follow in that last journey. They stood to view "afar off"; they watched the prophet go down to Jordan, they never, like Elisha, went through Jordan. They never walked and talked with Elijah beyond Jordan. They never beheld the chariot of fire, and horses of fire, nor did they see the prophet rapt to heaven by a whirlwind.

Nevertheless they recognise, with a measure of appreciation, the blessed effects upon the man that has seen these wonders. They bow themselves to the ground before him, and thus show that they see, in Elisha, one who moves on a higher spiritual level than themselves. They are willing to take the place of servants to one whom they recognise as servant of the Lord.

Are we not oftentimes like these men? We see that Christ has died for us; we are slow to accept His death as our death. We know perhaps little of a walk in communion with Him on resurrection ground, and what it is to behold Him as a living Man in the glory. Yet we can appreciate in others the effect of this personal intimacy with Christ. For there is no gainsaying the man who is characterized by the spirit of the Man that has gone to heaven. The world could take knowledge of Peter and John, "that they had been with Jesus"; and looking upon Stephen they "saw his face as it had been the face of an angel", and "were not able to resist the wisdom and the spirit by which he spake" (Acts 4:13; 6:10, 15).

Not only, however, were the sons of the prophets dull of heart, but they were slow of apprehension, and worse they were marked by unbelief. And yet withal they had a great show of natural strength: they have their "fifty strong men". But the thoughts of nature cannot rise above the mountains and valleys of earth. Only faith's trans-piercing gaze can see the vision of the man in heaven.

Thus unbelief is the first characteristic of the sphere in which Elisha is to be a witness; and this is found in those who make a religious profession. Nature cannot believe that the grace of God can take a man to heaven, though ready to suggest that the Spirit of God can take a man up to cast him down to earth. They knew, indeed, that Elijah was to be taken away, but apparently they did not believe that he was taken to heaven. They had knowledge, but they lacked faith. Elisha, ashamed of their unbelief, allows them to prove the vanity of their natural resources, by sending their fifty men on a fruitless three days search.

5. The Men of the City
2 Kings 2:19-22

The world in the midst of which Elisha is a witness to the grace of God is not only an unbelieving world, but, as the result of its unbelief, is a world under the curse. Very fittingly then Elisha's mission of grace commences at Jericho, the place of the curse. Joshua had said, "Cursed be the man before the Lord that riseth up and buildeth this city of Jericho: he shall lay the foundation thereof in his firstborn, and in his youngest son shall he set up the gates of it." So it came to pass, for in the days of Ahab, a man arose who defied the Lord by building Jericho, with the loss of his two sons "according to the word of the Lord that he spake by Joshua" (Joshua 6:26; 1 Kings 16:34).

The situation was pleasant, but the water was bad and the ground barren. Such is this world; at times outwardly fair, but over all the blight of the curse. Its sources of refreshment fail to satisfy. It promises much but brings nothing to fruition. It cannot meet the needs of man.

Elisha, however, is present with healing grace; a beautiful picture of Christ who, having nothing of this world's goods, yet dispenses blessing on every hand, using His grace for the good of others. The men of the city have faith to avail themselves of the grace that is in Elisha. They come to him with their need. The prophet asks for a new cruse and salt therein, speaking of the preserving character of grace linked, not with the flesh, but with a "new vessel". Was not Christ the "new vessel" filled with the preserving grace of God?

Then we read, Elisha "went forth unto the spring of the waters, and cast the salt in there, and said, Thus saith the Lord, I have healed these waters; there shall not be from thence any more death or barren land." So will it be in the days yet to come: in the very scene where the curse was pronounced, where the curse has fallen, there the curse will be removed. God will dwell with men—new vessels, made like to Christ filled with preserving grace. Then indeed there will be no more death nor curse, for the former things will have passed away.

6. The Mockers of Bethel
2 KINGS 2:23-25

In reading the story of Elisha it must ever be remembered that his mission was to present the grace of God to a guilty nation. For this reason his miracles are almost without exception miracles of grace. The three exceptions—the mocking youths who are cursed, Gehazi who is stricken with leprosy, and the death of the lord on whose hand the king leaned, are in perfect keeping with the prophet's mission. In every case the judgment is the direct outcome of slighting grace.

Thus while witness is given to God's sovereign grace in a number of striking miracles, there is also a witness to the inevitable judgment that will overtake those who reject, or falsify, or slight, the grace of God. At the beginning of his ministry Elisha has to learn that if he brings grace and blessing into the scene of the curse, he will be confronted by those who reject grace, and mock at the vessel of grace. Thus it comes to pass as the prophet went up to Bethel, he is met by a band of youths who mock at the ascension of Elijah. In derision they say to Elisha, "Go up, thou bald head; go up, thou bald head."

The sons of the prophets betray ignorance and unbelief as to the ascension. The "men of the city" may be indifferent to ascension, but the children of Bethel mock at ascension. In Bethel, the place that was distinguished in the history of Israel as the house of God, we find a band of mockers. Nor is it otherwise in this day of grace. There is still ignorance and unbelief in the religious circle, and indifference among the men of the world, but the most terrible mark of the last days will be the appearance of scoffers in the Christian profession—that which professes to be the house of God. For such there is nothing but judgment,—a judgment that begins at the house of God (2 Peter 3:3; 1 Peter 4:17).

Thus it was in the day of Elisha. The ascension of Elijah to heaven, the double portion of the spirit that rests on Elisha, the activities of grace for the blessing of man, are merely subjects for sport. The solemn result is that the one who is the minister of grace, invokes the judgment upon those who reject it.

7. The Kings and Their Armies
2 Kings 3

Hitherto Elisha has been the minister of grace in a limited circle: he now commences his public ministry in connection with the apostate nation. Through his intervention, three kings and their armies are saved from destruction, and a great victory gained over the enemies of God's people.

The whole scene vividly portrays the low and humiliating condition of the professing people of God. Jehoram, the king of the ten tribes, though putting away certain idols wrought evil in the sight of the Lord, and departed not from the sins of Jeroboam which made Israel to sin. In the government of God, Moab is allowed to rebel. To quell this rebellion Jehoram seeks the aid of the king of Judah. Jehoshaphat, himself a God-fearing man, falls into the snare. He abandons godly separation, enters into an unholy alliance with Jehoram, and thus sinks to the level of this wicked king. He joins with him to fight his battles, saying, "I will go up, I am as thou art, my people as thy people, and my horses as thy horses."

Moreover, both these kings—who profess the worship of Jehovah—are found in alliance with the heathen king of

Edom, an enemy of God. Thus we have the strange alliance of a wicked king, a God-fearing king, and a heathen king.

Without thought of God or reference to God, these three kings make their plans, and proceed to put them into practice. All seems to promise well until, at the end of seven days, they are confronted with circumstances that threaten their destruction, not by hand of the enemy, but from lack of water.

Stirred by an uneasy conscience, the king of Israel sees in these circumstances the hand of the Lord, who, he assumes, has called together these three kings to deliver them into the hands of Moab. If, however, the trial arouses the guilty fears of the apostate king, it also manifests the God-fearing character of the king of Judah. Both kings think of the Lord; one can only see in the trial that the Lord is against them in judgment; the other sees in the trial an occasion to turn to the Lord as their only resource. Jehoshaphat says, "Is there not here a prophet of the Lord, that we may enquire of the Lord by him?" Far better had he enquired of the Lord before starting on this expedition in company with the king of Israel. However, faced with the terrible circumstances, he is recalled to the Lord.

This enquiry brings Elisha to the front. The prophet's first words bear a bold witness against the wicked king of Israel, with whom he refuses to be associated, for, he asks, "What have I to do with thee?" This question is not only an exposure of the apostasy of the king of Israel, but a rebuke to the king of Judah, Jehoshaphat, a true saint, but who, walking according to the flesh, had formed an unholy alliance with Jehoram, and said, "I am as thou art, and my people as thy people." Elisha, walking according to the spirit of Elijah, refuses all association with Jehoram, saying, "What have I to do with thee?"

Doubtless, the king of Judah would never have consented to bow down with Jehoram before the golden calves. Nevertheless, he is ensnared into joining with one to fight the Lord's enemies with whom he cannot worship. Alas! how often in Christian days, has this scene been re-enacted. Under the plea of love, and helping in the service of the Lord, the believer has been drawn into association with those with whom he could not join in worship before the Lord. Such alliances set the blessing of men above the honour of the Lord. Are we not thus warned against the easy-going kindness of human nature that can at times betray us into thoughtlessly saying to those who are in a false position, "I am as thou art, my people as thy people"? Again does not this scene warn us to "Watch and pray, that ye enter not into temptation"? Not only to "watch" against the snares of the enemy, but to "pray", so that every step is taken in dependence upon God. It is well that we turn to God when a false step has plunged us into difficulty; but better far to walk in the spirit of prayer and dependence, and thus escape every crooked path.

Elisha, while refusing all association with Jehoram, and indirectly rebuking Jehoshaphat, does not hesitate to link himself with what is of God, and with the man that is in any little measure standing for God. He thus regards the presence of Jehoshaphat; otherwise he would not have looked toward the king of Israel, nor seen him.

None the less, the confusion caused by this unholy alliance between the two kings, is so great, that Elisha is hampered in discerning the mind of the Lord. Hence he calls for a minstrel. His mind must be diverted from all that is around him, and put in touch with heavenly scenes to know the Lord's mind. No minstrel was needed to condemn the apostate king of Israel, nor rebuke the folly and weakness of the king of Judah; when, however, it is a question of discerning the mind of heaven, then at once there is the need of the minstrel. The man of God must have his mind diverted from the utter confusion around, the destruction with which God's people are faced, and the consequent distress into which they are plunged. He cannot learn the mind of the Lord by dwelling upon the sorrowful circumstances. He is not indifferent to them; he does not ignore them; but if he is to learn how the Lord would have him to act he must be lifted above the distressing circumstances of an earthly scene into the serene calm of that heavenly scene into which Elijah had ascended, and from which Elisha had come forth to minister the sovereign grace of God in the midst of a ruined people.

In our own day, do we not at times need the minstrel—or that which the minstrel signifies? Are we not often faced with circumstances in which the evil is so apparent that it is easily detected, and condemned without any great call upon our spirituality? To discern, however, the mind of the Lord in the circumstances, demands far greater spirituality. For this we need to have our spirits withdrawn from the things of earth so that, undistractedly looking to the Lord, we may be able to see the condition of His people as He sees it, and thus gain His mind. The fact that it is easy to expose the evils that afflict the people of God, but difficult to find the remedy, only proves how much we need the minstrel—the abstraction of spirit from the confused issues amongst the people of God, that will alone enable us to learn the mind of the Lord.

Had Elisha only taken into account the wickedness of Jehoram, the failure of Jehoshaphat, and the distressing circumstances into which they were brought by this unholy alliance, he might have argued that the kings were only reaping what they had sown, and that evidently it was the Lord's mind that they should suffer a great defeat.

By the minstrel Elisha is lifted above the circumstances of God's people on earth into the calm of the Lord's presence in heaven, there to learn that the mind of the Lord is very different from what the mind of nature might expect. Elisha discovers that the Lord was going to use the occasion of His people's failure, and distress, to vindicate His own glory and magnify His grace. Not only would He preserve His people from the destruction that their own folly merited, but He would grant them a signal victory over their enemies. And thus it came to pass, the kings and their armies are saved, by God's gracious and miraculous intervention, and a great victory is gained over their enemies.

Nevertheless, it is well for us to note that, in spite of God's grace delivering His people from destruction, and giving them a victory over their enemies, *there is no revival Godward*. In Judah, there are indeed revivals Godward, as well as victories manward; but in all the sad history of Israel, though God may come to their help in their distress, there are no recorded revivals toward God.

8. The Widow's Oil

2 Kings 4:1-7

The God that "telleth the number of the stars", and "calleth them by their names", is the God that "healeth the broken in heart". The stars are too high, and the sorrows of a broken heart too deep, for us to reach: but the God that can count the myriad stars of heaven, can stoop to heal one broken heart on earth (Psalm 147:3, 4). The grace of God that has saved kings and their armies from destruction, is able to meet the need of one desolate widow. Elisha, too, the minister of this grace, is as ready to come to the help of this lowly widow as before he had been the willing servant of kings. If he saves the great ones of the earth in their difficulties, he will also save the poor in their distress.

The widow of a son of the prophets—one who feared the Lord—is threatened with the loss of her two sons to meet the claims of her creditor. That the widow of a prophet could be reduced to such straits is surely a solemn reflection on the low condition of the nation.

However, the woman has faith to avail herself of the grace that is ministered by Elisha. She spreads out her case before the prophet. He enquires, "What shall I do for thee? Tell me, what hast thou in the house?" Thus she is not only a woman with deep need, but it becomes manifest that her own resources are utterly insufficient to meet the need.

This surely is in harmony with the way of the Lord; for in His day, when the disciples tell Him of the need of the multitude, before exercising His grace, He makes manifest their utter inability to meet the case by asking, "How many loaves have ye?" The Lord's question brings to light that they had but five loaves and two small fishes. But what are they among so many? So Elisha's question brings to light that the widow has nothing in her house "save a pot of oil". But how can that save her from the claims of the creditor?

Such questions, whether on the part of the Master or the servant, prepare the way for the display of the grace of God. The Lord takes the five loaves and the two fishes and looking up to heaven blesses them. Thus having brought the disciples' little in touch with heaven's plenty, it more than meets the needs of the multitude. So with the widow's pot of oil: when brought into touch with the power of God in grace, it will more than meet her need.

Nevertheless, Elisha uses the pot of oil, even as the Lord uses the loaves and the fishes. In both cases they are provisions of God, and as such are not ignored. Another has said, "God does not allow us to be placed in circumstances which bear no evidence of His providing mercies. They may be very small and scanty, yet faith appropriates them, and encouraging the soul in God proclaims, 'The Lord is my helper', not *outside* His mercies, but *through* them." God had provided the widow with the personal means to meet her need, though she had to be directed how to use the means in dependence upon God. The neighbours can only provide the occasion to use the means at her disposal. Again it has been said, "The testimony in asking the loan of an empty vessel was that she, who was *known* to be in such abject circumstances, had something to put into them. She might doubtless have been taunted that her poverty was notorious, and that it was folly to borrow empty vessels. She had only boldly to say, 'The Lord is my helper.'" In using the means she must, however, shut the door upon all outside influences, and thus express her dependence upon God. Thus, while the grace of God comes in to meet her need, God does not ignore the gift with which she was endowed, small though it may be. In using it in dependence upon God she finds that it increases, with the result that her debts are paid and means provided for her living. Such is the mercy of God and the way it takes to meet our necessities. It was thus with the multitude in the Lord's day: their need was fully met, but the mercy of God was greater than their need. When all were filled there were still twelve baskets of fragments gathered up.

Moreover, has not this mystic scene an underlying spiritual meaning for believers? Here was one who wanted a blessing from God, and yet had nothing in her house save a pot of oil. Nevertheless, in the pot of oil there was the potential means provided by God to meet all her needs, and sustain her life. However, in order that God may use the oil, He needs empty vessels. The woman's part was to provide the empty vessels, and as long as she brings forth empty vessels, God will fill them. There was no lack in the supply of oil. The lack came on the woman's side. The oil stayed because there was not a vessel more.

Thus it is with the believer to-day who desires that all his spiritual needs may be met, and that he may enter upon the fulness of life. He has the power for this life in the gift of the Holy Spirit, of whom oil in Scripture is the constant type. There is the exhortation, "Be filled with the Spirit." However, to be filled with the Spirit, God must have empty vessels. There is oftentimes with us the allowance of unjudged flesh. The heart is filled with so much that is not Christ. The world in different degrees, and the flesh in varied forms, is allowed, and thus there is little room for the oil. We need to shut the door upon the world, and the flesh, in order that the Spirit that we possess may fill our hearts and, thus walking according to the Spirit and minding the things of the Spirit, we may find life and peace, "for the mind of the flesh is death; but the mind of the Spirit life and peace" (Romans 8:6, N.Tr.).

> *"What is our work when God a blessing would impart?*
> *To bring the empty vessel of a needy heart."*

Nor is the application of this incident limited to the individual. The Church, widowed by Christ's absence, fails to meet her responsibilities. Yet the Holy Ghost abides, and as we recognise His presence, and are subject to His ministry, we are enabled to face all our responsibilities, and as a result of God's operation live of the rest. All the fulness of the Godhead, as set forth in Christ in glory, is available for us.

9. The Shunammite
2 Kings 4:8-37

The beautiful story of the Shunammite was cast in a dark day in the history of Israel. The king of Israel "wrought evil in the sight of the Lord." The idols set up by Jeroboam were still worshipped by the people. The morally decadent nation was moving on to judgment.

In spite of the low state of the professing people of God, we are permitted to see that God was working in sovereign grace, through His servant Elisha, bringing to light a remnant that God had reserved to Himself, of whom the Shunammite is a shining example. Her story cannot fail to encourage believers who find themselves living in a yet darker day. On every hand the corrupt systems of Christendom are seeking to unite in a great worldly union in which every vital truth of Christianity will be lost, only to end in uniting into a lifeless mass to be spued out of Christ's mouth. Yet how good to know that in such a day God is working in sovereign grace, and still has His elect; little known by the world, but well known and recognised by God. As it was in the days of Elisha, and in the days of Malachi, so it has been in every dark day, and still is in these the darkest of all days—the closing days of Christendom.

In such days God observes, and listens to those who fear His name, and speak often one to another; and He keeps a book of remembrance for those that fear the Lord, and think upon His name. Thus it is that God has kept in remembrance for His praise, and our encouragement, the beautiful traits in the character of the Shunammite, that witness to the reality of her faith, and mark her off as one of God's elect.

She comes before us as a great woman of Shunem—a woman of wealth and position. None the less she was not ashamed to constrain a humble ploughman to enter her house to eat bread. She was not forgetful to entertain strangers. Her faith in God was proved by her hospitality to the servant of God, and she had her reward.

Moreover, there was with her spiritual discernment. She can say to her husband, of Elisha, "I perceive that this is an holy man of God." Blessed, indeed, that there should have been in Elisha the display of a character which marked him, in the eyes of others, as "an holy man of God"; blessed, too, that in the great woman of Shunem there was an appreciation of such a character. We may well covet both things—the Christian life so lived that all men can discern that we are disciples of Christ; and the deep appreciation of such a life when set forth in others. Does this not again bespeak the faith of God's elect? As we should say, "Whosoever believeth that Jesus is the Christ is born of God: and every one that loveth Him that begat loveth him also that is begotten of Him" (1 John 5:1).

Furthermore, her faith leads to practical service. It was no part of her work as a woman to go forth in public service, but she did what she could. She uses her means to make provision in private, for one that God was using in public. Moreover, she does so in a way that proves she had right spiritual instincts. She knew what was suited to one who witnessed against the wickedness of men, and testified to the grace of God. Therefore it is that she does not make provision for the prophet according to the resources of her wealth, and the rich appointments that would be natural to a great woman. She only provides that which would be suited to the simple tastes and needs of "an holy man of God". "A little chamber" with simple furnishings—a bed, a table, a stool, and a candlestick—she felt would be in accord with the mind of one who was apart from the world and its ways, and who had been in touch with heavenly scenes.

Thus it is she meets the need of the prophet; but she does so without ostentation. She entertains according to the needs and tastes of her guest, and with no thought of exalting herself in the eyes of her guest by making a parade of her wealth. In the "little chamber" there was no provision to meet the lust of the eye, the lust of the flesh and the pride of life; but there was all necessary provision to meet the need of a heavenly stranger.

And this perception of his tastes, and provision for his needs, is duly appreciated by the prophet, who gladly avails himself of her kindness. Furthermore, Elisha will show that he is not unmindful of her goodness, and would fain make some recompense. He has just been the instrument of saving kings, captains, and their armies from an overwhelming catastrophe, and doubtless, at the moment, could have obtained favours from high quarters. Would then this great woman like Elisha to speak to the king, or captain of the host, on her behalf? Her answer is very beautiful, and gives further proof that she is imbued with the spirit of God's elect. She says, "I dwell among mine own people." She is satisfied to be outside the high circles of a corrupt world, and has no desire for its distinctions and favours. She would fain pursue her retired way with her *own people*, content to be unknown by the great ones of the earth. Happy for us, if belonging to that privileged heavenly company, that the Lord recognises as *"His own"* we take a place outside this world, not fearing its frowns, nor courting its favours, and whole-heartedly identify ourselves with that company as our *"own company"* (John 13:1; Acts 4:23).

Elisha, however, has other resources to draw upon than the kings and captains of this world. He is in touch with higher powers and heavenly courts. He can draw upon the mighty power of God "who quickeneth the dead". Blessing from this heavenly source the woman will not refuse, though, at the moment, what Elisha proposes, seems almost beyond her faith. However, in due time, she learns like the wife of Abraham, in a day that was past, and the wife of Zacharias, in a day yet to come, that God can quicken the dead, and that what He has promised He is able to perform. So it comes to pass; in due season, she embraces a son.

There is, however, another and a deeper lesson she has to learn. Through experience, trying indeed to the flesh, she will discover that the life-giving God is also the God of resurrection. Had not Abraham to learn this lesson on Mount Moriah? And have we not also to learn that God is not only the Quickener who gives life, He is also the God of resurrection that can give back life when death has shewn its power? To learn this lesson, Abraham, in his day, had to bind Isaac to the altar on Mount Moriah, and the woman must face the death of her beloved child. So it came to pass when the child was grown, there came a day when he was stricken down in the field and was carried to the mother to die in her arms.

This sore trial very blessedly brings out the faith of the Shunammite. In perfect calmness she lays the dead child on the bed of the man of God, and shutting the door upon him went out. She utters no word of what has happened to her husband, but simply calls upon him to supply her with a young man, and one of the asses, to go to the man of God. The one who was the instrument to give life is the one to whom she turns in the presence of death.

Her husband, ignorant of what has happened, asks, "Wherefore wilt thou go to him to-day? It is neither new moon, nor sabbath." If he thinks of the man of God, it is only in connection with new moons and sabbaths. Like many another, in this day, his only thought of God is connected with a religious festival, or the outward observance of a day. The links that faith has with God are matters of life and death. Faith, however, may not be able to argue with unbelief, or meet the questions raised by mere reason; but faith can say in the darkest moment, "It is well" (N.Tr.). Thus the faith of the Shunammite, rising above the sorrow that filled her mother's heart, knowing that the dead child is lying in the prophet's chamber, and in the face of all the questions of unbelief, can say, *"It is well."*

Having obtained the servant and the ass, she hastens to the man of God. Elisha, seeing her coming, sends Gehazi to meet her. To all his enquiries she has but one answer, "It is well"; but she will not unburden her heart to the servant. Pressing on to the man of God she flings herself at his feet uttering a few broken sentences that reveal to Elisha the cause of her trouble.

Immediately Elisha sends Gehazi with his staff to lay upon the face of the child. However, this does not satisfy the woman: her faith clings to the man of God. Her faith refused to be hindered by her husband, with his talk of new moons and sabbaths, from going to the man of God; and now that she has come she will not leave the man of God by reason of Gehazi and the staff. Thus it is she says, "As the Lord liveth, and as thy soul liveth, I will not leave thee." She rightly feels that servants and staves will be of no avail. Nothing but the power of God brought in by one who is in touch with God will restore the dead child.

Her spiritual instincts are right. The prophet goes with her, and on the way the servant meets them with the news that the staff has accomplished nothing.—"The child is not awakened." Arrived at the house, the prophet finds that "the child is dead, and laid upon the bed." He went into the chamber of death and "shut the door upon them twain and prayed unto the Lord." It was a solemn moment in which the prophet felt his utter dependence upon the Lord; and more, he felt the deep necessity of being alone with the Lord. The husband, with his talk of new moons and sabbaths; the servant, with his staff, and the woman with her sorrow, must all be shut out. Religious observances will not bring the child back; the staff, that may meet every day circumstances, will be of no avail in this sore strait; grief, however real will not recall the child. It must be the Lord alone who can raise the dead. Thus it is that Elisha, "shut the door … and prayed unto the Lord."

Furthermore, the prophet identifies himself with the one for whom he prays. He "lay upon the child, and put his mouth upon his mouth, and his eyes upon his eyes, and his hands upon his hands: and he stretched himself upon the child."

Do we not see in this fine scene, the effectual fervent prayer of a righteous man? Prayer which rightly excluded everything of man and his efforts—prayer that looks only to the Lord, and wholly identifies itself with the need of the one for whom prayer is made. Such faith has its reward—the prayer is answered, for we read, "the flesh of the child waxed warm." Yet, even so, it was not without the wrestling of faith, and the agony of prayer, for we read that the prophet "returned, and *walked in the house to and fro;* and went up and stretched himself upon him." Then the child opened his eyes.

The prophet having sent for the Shunammite says, with becoming calmness, "Take up thy child." The woman on her part, expresses no amazement, but, in thankfulness "fell" at the prophet's feet, "bowed herself to the ground, and took up her son and went out."

God is not unmindful of this simple, unquestioning faith that clings to God, even when death has closed all earthly hopes, and put the child beyond all human aid. Thus it comes to pass, that amongst God's worthies, who have obtained a good report by faith, we read, "Women received their dead raised to life again" (Hebrews 11:35).

In answer to the faith of the woman, and the prayers of Elisha, God reveals Himself as, not only One who gives life where life had never been before; but also as the God who quickens and calls back to life one who has been into death. So, too, it is our high privilege to know God, revealed in Christ according to the Lord's own words, "I AM THE RESURRECTION AND THE LIFE."

10. The Time of Dearth
2 KINGS 4:38-41

Each changing scene in Elisha's eventful history increasingly discloses the ruin of Israel, only to make manifest that where sin abounds grace does much more abound. Already we have seen the curse at Jericho, scoffers at Bethel, Moab in rebellion, widows in need; and now we find "there was a dearth in the land".

In this time of famine Elisha comes to Gilgal. The sons of the prophets are found sitting before Elisha; suggesting that in their dire need they are waiting upon the man of God to bring relief. They rightly assume that the one who had saved armies from destruction, and raised the dead child of the Shunammite, had resources to meet their need in a time of famine. With the sons of the prophets there was faith to use the grace of God ministered through the prophet. God delights to answer faith, however feeble, and will never fail those who wait upon Him: though He may take a way which, while meeting our needs, will disclose to us our weakness.

Thus it comes to pass that Elisha instructs his servant to "set on the great pot and seethe pottage" for those who were looking to him for provision. It would seem that, in this time of dearth, they had been naturally husbanding their slender resources by using some smaller vessel. Nature would argue that the prevailing dearth would only require a little pot. Providence would suggest that a wise economy demanded the little pot. With God, however, there is no lack of supply; and faith, bringing God in, calls for "the great pot". Earth's shortage is best met with a little pot: heaven's plenty is only met by "the great pot". We can count upon great things from a great God.

The directions to seethe pottage were given by the prophet to his servant. However, there was one present to whom no directions were given, and who must needs intermeddle with the servant's work: one who was not content, as were the sons of the prophets, to sit before Elisha, but with restless activity must go "out into the field" at his own charges, and seek to help in meeting the common need by adding his contribution to the pot.

If we are to partake of heaven's provision we must needs be in quiet rest in the presence of Christ, like the sons of the prophets sitting before Elisha. So in later days the place of rich provision was found by Mary sitting at the feet of Jesus, rather than by Martha with her restless activity. Doubtless the man who "went into the field to gather herbs", was a very sincere man and thought, as Martha in her day, that he was contributing to the general good. It was, however, the intrusion of the flesh in Gilgal, the very place that signified the cutting off of the flesh. The result was that through the fleshly zeal of one man, death is brought into the pot.

This man, leaving the presence of Elisha, goes out into the field to gather herbs. He thought to add something from the field to the supply that Elisha was drawing from heaven. The field in Scripture is ever used as a picture of the cultured world. The culture of this world can add nothing to the food from heaven. The Colossians, in their day, were in danger of seeking to supplement Christianity by the addition of human eloquence, human philosophy and human superstition. They were adding wild gourds to the heavenly pottage. Instead of bringing the soul into closer relationships with God, such efforts end in separating the soul from God.

Moreover, there is no difficulty in securing wild gourds. It was a time of dearth, and yet with the greatest ease this man gathered "his lap full". There may have been a dearth of wholesome life-sustaining food, there was no dearth of wild gourds.

The mischief is at once detected when the pottage is poured out. All the company detect the poison. Had it been one man who complained of the pottage, it might have been suggested that his taste was at fault. But we read, "As *they* were eating of the pottage, that *they* cried out, and said, O man of God, there is death in the pot. And *they* could not eat thereof." That which should have been a source of supply to maintain life, had become, by one man's act, a means to destroy life. They may not know how to meet the difficulty; but at least they are alive to the trouble, and, moreover, they rightly turn to the man of God for guidance.

Their appeal to Elisha is not in vain, for he has resources to meet this fresh need. He has an antidote for the poison. His simple instructions are, "bring meal", which at once is cast into the pot with the result there was no longer any harm in the pot. Does not this meal speak of Christ? The thoughts of nature, the philosophy of man, the elements of the world, the religion of the flesh—things by which man seeks to add something to God's provision to meet His people's need—are all exposed and corrected by the presentation of Christ. It was thus the Apostle met the attempt to introduce wild gourds that threatened the Colossian saints. The Apostle detects the poison—the enticing words of the moralist, the philosophy and vain deceit of the world, the insistence of the holy days, of the new moons, and of sabbath days, by the ritualist; and the worshipping of angels by the superstitious. To meet these poisonous influences that are destructive of the true life of Christianity he presents Christ. He says all these things "are not after Christ". They may be served up with "enticing words" and "much shew of wisdom" and apparent "humility", but they "are not after Christ". Then he presents Christ in all His glory as the Head of the Assembly—His body. As it were, he casts the meal into the pot. He tells us that we have all we need in Christ, for "in Him dwelleth all the fulness of the Godhead", and further, "we are complete in Him." "Christ is all and in all" (Colossians 2, 3).

11. The Multitude Fed
2 Kings 4:42-44

In this time of dearth, a man comes from Baal-shalisha with twenty loaves of barley, and full ears of corn in a sack, as a gift of firstfruits to the man of God. Immediately Elisha says, "Give unto the people, that they may eat." Freely he had received and freely he gives. He does not keep for his own use that which had been freely given to him. In giving the gift increases, so that, not only his own need is met, but the needs of one hundred men are met, and more than met.

The servant of the prophet cannot understand how twenty loaves can meet the need of one hundred men; but again Elisha's word is, "Give the people that they may eat." He says, as it were, if you will but give in accordance with the word of the Lord, you will find there will be enough to meet the need of the people and to spare. Nature raises questions and says, How can this be? It is told not to reason but only obey and all will be well.

So, in the day of the Lord, the natural reasoning of the human mind in Judas, can ask, "How is it?" in the presence of communications that transcend all human thought. Such reasoning is met, not with any explanation that would

THE MULTITUDE FED

gratify human reason, but with the Lord's words that "If a man love Me he will *keep My* words"; and this would lead to the realization of things that are beyond human explanation. Judas would fain reason in order to understand, but is told to obey in order to realize. In like manner Elisha meets the "how" of the amazed and reasoning servant. He must act upon the word of the Lord, and he will realize the blessing of the Lord, even if he cannot explain the power and grace of the Lord.

So it came to pass; "he set it before them, and they did eat, and left thereof, according to the word of the Lord." The prophet gives of that which had been freely given to him, the servant obeys, the need is met, and the gift has so increased that after every need is met there is "left thereof, according to the word of the Lord."

For we must share, if we would keep,
That good thing from above;
Ceasing to give, we cease to have—
Such is the law of Love.

12. The Healing of the Leper
2 KINGS 5:1-19

Hitherto Elisha has been the minister of the grace of God in the midst of Israel; now he becomes a means of blessing to one outside the nation. Grace is extended to a Gentile.

The whole scene would seem to be a foreshadowing of the present dispensation, in which Israel is set aside and governmental power is given to the Gentiles. The times of the Gentiles are prefigured by the fact the Lord had given deliverance to the Syrians—the open enemy of Israel, and that captives had been taken from Israel. The power had passed to the Gentile, and an Israelitess is in captivity. During this time the Lord shows grace to the Gentile.

In Naaman we see man at his best estate. Socially he was "a great man"; officially he was a successful man; personally he was a brave man. Such was Naaman before the world. Nevertheless, the one who is the favourite of the king, and the hero of the people, is pronounced by God to be a leper. In a twofold way leprosy is a fitting type of sin. The loathsomeness of the disease sets forth the defiling character of sin, constituting man a sinner in nature. The incurable character of the disease, sets forth the hopeless condition to which sin reduces a man. As fallen men we are

THE HEALING OF THE LEPER

not only sinful in nature, but also without strength to change our state. If we are to be blessed, we are shut up to the grace of God. Thus the word runs, "By grace are ye saved, through faith ... not of works" (Ephesians 2:8, 9).

Thus his disease, coupled with his helpless condition, constituted Naaman a fitting object for God's sovereign grace and mercy. That which gave Naaman such a great place before the world had no value in God's sight. The Lord, who, in His day (Luke 4:27), uses Naaman as an illustration of grace reaching a Gentile, does not say there were many great men, and honourable men, and men of valour. None of these qualities would have made men suited objects for grace: therefore He says, there were "many lepers".

Further, in this fine scene, we see not only the activity of grace to a sinner, but the way God takes to make known this grace. He takes a way that pours contempt on all our pride. He has "chosen the foolish things of the world, that He may put to shame the wise; and God has chosen the weak things of the world, that He may put to shame the strong things; and the ignoble things of the world, and the despised has God chosen, and things that are not that He may annul the things that are; so that no flesh should boast before God." In consistency with these ways of God we pass at once from "a great man" to "a little maid"—a stranger in a strange land, and in the lowly position of a slave to Naaman's wife. God is going to bless one who, in the sight of the world, is "a great man", and hence He will use in this work of grace "a little maid". However, if her position in this world was insignificant, if she was "little", her faith was great. For she can say, "Would God my lord were with the prophet that is in Samaria! for *he would recover him of his leprosy.*" This surely is the language of faith. There is no suggestion that he might be able to ameliorate the trouble, and possibly effect a cure; but with the boldness and certainty of faith she says, "He would recover him of his leprosy." She speaks as one who knows the healing power of grace. Naaman, as it has been said, may feel the sore; the little maid knew the healing. Her confidence is the more remarkable since she could not, in her experience, have seen any case of the healing of the leper; for the Lord, Himself, says, that in the time of Elisha, there were many lepers but *"none of them was cleansed"* saving Naaman the Syrian.

The word of the little maid does its work. It awakens the desire for the blessing in the heart of the needy Naaman. However, the ways of grace cannot be understood by the natural man. Filled with his own thoughts, he pays but little heed to the word of the little maid. She with her knowledge of the grace and power of God speaks of the prophet in Samaria; he, following his natural thoughts, turns to the king of Syria, thinking that the coveted blessing can be secured through the great ones of the earth, aided by the payment of a great fee.

The king of Syria sets forth man in his self esteem. He is only too pleased that his servant Naaman should have the blessing, but he would fain be the channel by which he obtains the blessing. So he says, "Go to, go, and I will send a letter to the king of Israel." One king will write to another king. But God does not require, and will not brook the patronage of kings. Grace is available for the guilty, whether that guilty one be amongst the exalted in the land or among the lowly—"a great man" or "a little maid"—but the patronage of kings cannot secure it, and gold cannot buy it.

However, Naaman has to prove that all these human efforts to secure the blessing leave him in a worse plight. So he comes to the king of Israel with his gifts and the letter from the king of Syria. The king of Israel realizes that this is a case

THE HEALING OF THE LEPER

for God alone, but he is ignorant of the man of God through whom the grace of God is being ministered. Without faith in God, and ignorant of the man of God, he can only conclude that the king of Syria is seeking an occasion for a quarrel by demanding that which is beyond the power of man to grant. Naaman discovers the hopelessness of turning to a man of the world, but, even so, it does not occur to Naaman to go to the prophet. It would seem then that all is over, and Naaman must return to Syria uncleansed and unblessed.

At this juncture, however, Elisha acts, and it becomes plain that if Elisha had not spoken, Naaman would never have come to the prophet, even though at the outset he had heard of the prophet. Nor is it otherwise with the sinner and Christ. We may indeed hear of Christ, but it is written, "No man can come to Me, except the Father which hath sent Me draw him" (John 6:44): and again, "No man can come unto Me, except it were given unto him of my Father" (John 6:65).

As a result of Elisha's intervention, Naaman, earnestly desiring the blessing, comes to the prophet. At last he has come to the right man; but he has come in the wrong way. He is not yet in the right condition to receive the blessing. He comes with his horses and chariots and stands at the door of the house of Elisha. Horses and chariots speak of the pomp and pride of man. Naaman has found that the might of kings can effect nothing, that money and gifts are of no avail; he must now learn that his own greatness and importance will not secure him the slightest notice on the part of God, with whom there is no respect of persons. Hence while he hears the message that, if received and obeyed, will bring salvation to him, yet no account is made of the greatness of Naaman. Elisha does not look at him as a great man, or honourable, or valiant; he simply sees in him a leper that needs cleansing. Elisha makes nothing of all the pomp and grandeur of Naaman; nor does he seek to exalt himself by this important visitor. He simply sends a message. This, indeed, is still the preacher's work, to deliver a message.

Nature, however, rebels against such treatment. The pride of man would like to have some consideration. But if Naaman is to receive the blessing it can be only on the ground of grace, and grace recognises no merit in the recipient of grace, otherwise it would not be grace. Hence it is that sovereign grace is so offensive to the natural man. "Naaman was wroth", and the real hindrance to his receiving blessing is discovered to be that he had thoughts of his own. "I thought" is the trouble. He thought he would only have to sit in his chariot and that Elisha would come and *stand* before Naaman, and add dignity to the scene by calling upon the name of the Lord his God, with a few passes of his hand up and down, and lo, he would be healed.

Further, Naaman objects to washing in Jordan. If it is a question of washing in a river, surely the larger rivers of his own country—Abana and Pharpar—are better than all the waters of Israel. Thus it is with many a sinner to-day, who admits the need of a moral change in the life, but not of a new birth. Men will submit to reformation effected by human means, but are not prepared to be set aside in the death of Christ. Naaman had expected some dramatic scene—to have some fuss made over him—and lo, this prince among men, is put off with a curt message. He is told, as any poor man might be, to go and bathe seven times in the public stream of Jordan. The whole thing appeared too commonplace for the high and mighty Naaman. The message ignored all his greatness; placed him on a level with the most insignificant person in the land, and told him to take a course that was open to any peasant. Elisha could not have treated the lowest in the land with less consideration.

THE HEALING OF THE LEPER

Such treatment, and such a message, were intolerable to the great man. "So he turned and went away in a rage."

Well, if he must go away, it is better to go in a rage, for at least it shows he was deeply stirred. Better thus than those who politely refuse God's grace with a "Pray Thee have me excused." For such there is no hope; God excuses them, and it is all over with the man that God excuses. For the man that goes away in a rage there is hope that he will return in more chastened mood, for at least he is in earnest.

Naaman had expected some great display, and nature craves for the dramatic, the sensational and the emotional; but Naaman must learn, as every sinner, that the mighty power of the gospel is not in "the earthquake, nor in the fire, but in the still small voice" of the word of God speaking to the conscience.

Happily for Naaman there were those around him who could plead with him and convince him of his folly. The little maid had borne her witness, the prophet had delivered his message—so simple and definite; now "his servants come near" and plead with him about the message. There are those to-day who do the work of the little maid—they invite to the preaching. There are those who deliver the message—the proclamation of the gospel. There are those who plead with the anxious soul individually, so that difficulties and hindrances to receiving the gospel may be removed. Thus with affectionate interest the servants plead with their master. "My father," they say, "if the prophet had bid thee do some great thing, wouldest thou not have done it? how much rather then, when he saith to thee wash and be clean?" How well these servants knew their master; he was a great man, and all his life had been doing great things. He had acquired a great position in the kingdoms of men by doing great things; but if, as we should say, he is to enter the kingdom of heaven, he must be converted and become as a little child. And thus it came to pass: the pleadings of the servants prevail, for we read, "Then went he down." His pride, his greatness, his valour, all that he was as a natural man is given up as a means of obtaining the blessing. Kings and their great gifts are left behind: Abana and Pharpar are forgotten, and, in the obedience of faith, he went down and dipped seven times in Jordan "according to the saying of the man of God". Such an act m the eyes of the world would seem the height of folly, even as the preaching of the Cross is foolishness to the wise men of this world. Jordan signifies death, and is used, in this scene, as a type of the death of Christ meeting the holiness of God. If the sinner is to be cleansed from his guilt it can only be on the ground of the death of Christ. In type Naaman owns this perfectly, without reserve, by dipping seven times in Jordan. He owns there is no cleansing except through the waters of death under which he is brought by the obedience of faith.

Thus it is with the sinner to-day. The blessing can only come to us in grace through the death and resurrection of Christ, and we pass under the efficacy of that death through faith in Christ. The Israelite, like Naaman, was originally "a Syrian ready to perish" (Deuteronomy 26:5), and for him Jordan meant the close of one phase of life (wilderness life), and the introduction to another sphere of life. The Jordan was the boundary of Syrian territory. Death ends the link with the Syrian. By dipping in Jordan Naaman in type ends the old life, and begins an entirely new life; his flesh becomes as the flesh of a little child. His former state as a leper, in which corruption and death were operating, was wholly unsuited to God; debarring him from God's presence. This was met by the waters of death. An evil nature cannot be forgiven, it must be ended by death. So with the

THE HEALING OF THE LEPER

believer, the old nature is condemned and done with in the death of Christ. The soul that, in the obedience of faith, submits to God's way of deliverance enters upon a new life.

The prophet emphasises the importance of this lesson by prescribing it seven times, setting forth how thoroughly we need to learn the lesson of our death with Christ, so bringing to an end the state in which we lived to ourselves in order that, in newness of life we may live to God.

The result for Naaman was that his flesh came again like unto the flesh of "a little child". What a marvellous change! The man who at the beginning of the story is described as "a great man", in the end becomes like "a little child". Moreover, a new spirit possessed him. The pride of a great man has given place to the lowliness of a little child; for, we read, "He returned to the man of God, he and all his company, and *stood* before him." He is no longer a great man sitting in his chariot, but a humble man standing before the prophet.

This, however, is not all. He has believed in his heart; now he confesses with his mouth, "There is no God in all the earth, but in Israel." Not only is he cleansed, but he is brought to know God. "I know" he can say. The gospel that meets our need, reveals God to our souls.

Then he would fain express his gratitude to the one through whom he has been so richly blessed. Elisha refuses the gift lest in any way he might appear to falsify the grace of God in the eyes of this Gentile, who had received the blessing without money and without price. Naaman, the possessor of great wealth, had doubtless acquired the habit of thinking that anything could be purchased with the power of money. He has to learn, even as the sinner to-day, that there are blessings beyond all other blessings, and joys beyond all earthly joys, and the life that is eternal, that all the riches of this world cannot purchase; though alas! they may block the way that leads to life and blessing.

Furthermore, the heart of Naaman goes out in worship to the Lord. He says, "Thy servant will henceforth offer neither burnt offering nor sacrifice unto other gods, but unto the Lord."

Lastly the change in his life is shown by his exercised and tender conscience. He at once felt that the worship of the Lord was wholly inconsistent with bowing down before an idol in the house of Rimmon. Yet his official position would possibly require that he should enter the idol's house. In answer to this difficulty Elisha's word is "Go in peace." This by no means implied that Elisha sanctioned Naaman's bowing down to the idol in the house of Rimmon. He saw that Naaman was exercised before the Lord, and without anticipating the difficulty, he knows he can safely leave Naaman with the Lord. We may be sure that Naaman never entered the house of Rimmon.

13. The Servant of the Prophet
2 KINGS 5:20-27

Now and again there pass before us in Scripture those who lie and deceive: but there is no more deliberate liar than Gehazi. As with Ananias and Sapphira, so with Gehazi, covetousness was the root of the lying.

The wealth of Naaman—the ten talents of silver, the six thousand pieces of gold, the ten changes of raiment—had stirred up the unjudged covetousness in the heart of Gehazi. The need of Naaman drew forth the grace of God in the prophet; the wealth of Naaman drew forth the covetousness of his servant. The grace of God had brought blessing to Naaman; the covetousness of Gehazi would belie the grace of God. A rich man willing and delighted to bestow a handsome gift, was too good an opportunity for a covetous man to let pass.

To gratify his greed, Gehazi does not hesitate to act lies as well as tell lies. He runs after Naaman and says, "My master hath sent me." This was the first lie. Then he invents the story of the visit of the two young men of Ephraim—a second lie. Having obtained two talents of silver, and two changes of raiment, he returns with two of Naaman's servants to help him carry the gift as far as the hill (not "tower" as in the Authorised Version). To go further would be to come into view of Elisha's house; so he pauses at the hill, and lets the men go. Having hidden the goods in the house, "He went in, and stood before his master" as if nothing had happened. He acts a lie. When asked by Elisha, where he had been, he attempts to cover his former lies by telling another lie, "Thy servant went no whither." One lie leads to other lies.

Then follows the solemn exposure. The whole terrible sin, in all its detail, was known to the prophet: but more, the motive that prompted the sin was known. Hidden in Gehazi's heart was the desire to acquire social position as a possessor of oliveyards, vineyards, sheep, oxen, menservants and maidservants.

Lastly the exposure is followed by the judgment. If Gehazi had taken of Naaman's wealth, he must also take Naaman's disease. He had acquired two changes of raiment from Naaman by lying and deceit; he also obtains a change of skin by the judgment of God. And the leprosy that he acquires will cling to him all the days of his life. The wealth he has obtained will soon be spent, the leprosy will abide. No waters of Jordan will cleanse Gehazi.

He came in before his master as a liar; he went out from his presence a leper as white as snow. In grasping at the wealth of Naaman, he inherits the disease of Naaman, and loses his place as the servant of the prophet. Once more he appears in the court of the king, but no more as the servant of Elisha.

In estimating the sin of Gehazi, the prophet first looks at it in connection with God and His grace. How will his act affect the testimony of God? He sees that Gehazi's sin presents an entirely false view of the grace of God. Elisha had been careful to refuse Naaman's gifts, lest this Gentile should think that the blessings of God can be obtained by gifts. Gehazi's sin would tend to nullify this testimony to the freeness of the grace of God. It was no "time" to receive gifts.

Are we not warned by this solemn scene that if we allow *unjudged* lust or covetousness in our hearts, we shall be ready to fall into temptation when it crosses our path. Further, one sin leads to another. We cannot stop just according to our own will in the path of sin. As one has said, "A man cannot stop his boat at will in the strong currents just above Niagara, though he might have avoided them altogether."

Then it is obvious that great religious advantages will not, of themselves, protect against grievous sin. Who could have had greater advantages than Gehazi? He lived with one of the greatest prophets the world has known—one who, again and again, is described as a man of God—and yet Gehazi fell. "Let him that thinketh he standeth, take heed lest he fall."

Finally we learn that the pursuit of sin destroys all sense of the presence and power of God. Gehazi must have had repeated experiences of the power of the man of God to read men's hearts and discern the motives of their actions. No one knew better than Gehazi this power of God that was with the prophet. Nevertheless, while Gehazi is seeking to gratify his covetous heart, it is so absorbed with the overruling passion of greed that, for the time, he entirely loses all sense of the presence of the omniscient God.

Thus, with the judgment of God upon him Gehazi goes out from the presence of the prophet, as in the day to come a yet greater sinner will go out from the presence of the Lord into the night, and Ananias and Sapphira will fall dead under the judgment of the Holy Spirit.

14. The Borrowed Axe
2 Kings 6:1-7

Once again the story of Elisha passes from kings and great men, to a simple domestic scene connected with the building of a dwelling place for the sons of the prophets. The incident very happily displays the simplicity and lowliness of life that marked this man of God. He is ready to meet the difficulties of kings and their armies, and, in due season, can concern himself with felling a tree and building a house. With the utmost ease he can deal with a great man of the world, and with like ease he can accommodate himself to the simple affairs of the lowly sons of the prophets. In the greatness of his way he can stoop to small affairs and walk with humble folk.

In like spirit the great Apostle, of the Christian day, can carry the burdens of the Church and work at making a tent; can save hundreds of souls from a watery grave, and help to pick up sticks to make a fire. And may we not say, that both these great servants are but showing forth the spirit of their yet greater Lord and Master, who, while bearing up the whole universe, can take a little child into His arms, and, though dwelling in the bosom of the Father, can enter the humble home of a fisherman.

Moreover, in the simple acts of these servants it is made manifest what power was at their disposal. Contrary to all human experience, the venomous beast that attacks the Apostle when picking up sticks, is shaken into the fire without resulting harm. And contrary to all natural laws the axe head is made to swim upon the waters. Thus the very laws of nature are reversed, or held in abeyance, in order to relieve the distress of the man with the borrowed axe. God, the Creator of the laws that govern creation, can alter His laws in order to manifest the grace that enables Peter to walk upon the water in the day of the Lord, and the iron to swim upon the water in the day of the prophet.

The very way in which the iron is made to swim makes manifest the power of God; for what relation can we see between cause and effect—between casting a stick into the stream and the swimming of the iron? May there not be underneath this simple story some deeper spiritual lesson? We see the power of the river overcome by the piece of wood cast into the waters. Seeing that Jordan is a type of death, this striking incident may well signify the power of death overcome by the Cross, and the House of God built by that which comes out of death.

15. The Syrian Raids
2 Kings 6:8-23

Elisha, having used the grace of God to relieve a distressed individual, now becomes the instrument of grace to save a guilty nation. The prophet, who had rebuked the king of Israel for his unbelief in connection with the letter from the king of Syria, now warns the king of the secret plans by which the king of Syria seeks his destruction. Thus the grace of God intervenes to save the king of Israel, "not once nor twice", by the hand of one who knows how to rebuke and when to warn.

The king of Syria, learning that his plans are frustrated, not by any traitor, but, by Elisha, sends horses, chariots and a great host, to take him captive. The fact that he sends a great host to take one man, proves in a striking way that the ungodly realize their weakness, and helplessness, in the presence of one man sustained by the power of God. So the wicked Ahab felt in an earlier day, when he sent his captains with their fifties to take the solitary Elijah; as even so in a later day, when the Jews sent a band of officers and men to take the Lord of glory. The world instinctively knows that one man, if God is with him, is stronger than a great host without God.

THE SYRIAN RAIDS

To natural sight Elisha's case seemed hopeless. The Syrians had taken every precaution. The great host had exercised all care by approaching Dothan under cover of darkness, and had succeeded in compassing about the city. There seemed no way of escape for the prophet. Thus the servant of Elisha, looking at things seen, exclaims, "Alas my master! how shall we do?"

Elisha quietens the young man's alarm. He says, "Fear not: for they that be with us are more than they that be with them." The young man is walking by sight: Elisha is walking by faith. The prophet anticipates the experience of the Apostle who can say, "If God be for us who can be against us?"

Elisha, however, is not content to rest in quiet faith himself, nor seek only to comfort others. He would fain bring the young men to his own spiritual elevation. Realizing that only God can accomplish this, he prays to the Lord to open his servant's eyes. His prayer is answered; "The Lord opened the eyes of the young man." There was no need for Elisha to have his eyes opened. He had already seen the chariots of Israel and the horsemen thereof waiting upon Elijah as he ascended from earth to heaven. The faith of the prophet realizes that the same chariots and horses of God accompany him as he takes his journey through the earth. The young man has seen the horses and chariots, with the great host, that encompassed the city, now he sees the mountain "full of horses and chariots of fire round about Elisha." The Syrian host may be round about the city, but what can they do if God's high host is round about Elisha? Paul may be surrounded with enemies who would kill him, and a raging storm that would engulf him, but what harm can touch him if the angel of the Lord stands by him? (Acts 27:23). The host against Elisha may be mighty, but the host of God is mightier. "The chariots of God are twenty thousand, even thousands of angels." Good too for us if we take our journey, through a hostile world, in the blessed consciousness of faith that One is with us who has said, "I will never leave thee, nor forsake thee"; and that we are in the providential care of those angel hosts who have been "sent forth to minister to them who shall be heirs of salvation."

Further, we are permitted to see that Elisha deals with the enemies of God according to the ways of grace, while, at the same time, manifesting that they are completely in his power. Thus it comes to pass that while the young man had his eyes opened, the enemies of God's prophet will now have their eyes blinded. It was so spiritually when the Lord was here, for He came "that they which see not might see; and that they which see might be made blind" (John 9:39). To own one's blindness and submit to God is the way to sight, as the blind man of John's Gospel found.

These blinded Syrians come completely under the power of Elisha, who leads them into Samaria. Then, when their eyes are opened, they discover they are captives—led captive by the very man they had set out to take. But if Elisha is in touch with the power of God, he is also the exponent of the mercy of God. The Syrians realize that as far as they are concerned their case is hopeless. They who once had encompassed the little city of Dothan are now themselves surrounded in the stronghold of their enemy. When it is thus made manifest that nothing but mercy can save them from destruction, they become the recipients of mercy. Not only are they saved but "great provision" is set before them; and when they had eaten they are sent away to their master. They are brought to realize that, "It is of the Lord's mercies that we are not consumed" (Lamentations 3:22). Such are the blessed ways of God's grace.

The man who has for his protection a mountain full of horses and chariots of fire—who is encompassed about with the mighty power of God—can afford to show mercy to those who are completely in his power. The man of nature, with no such resources of power, cannot risk showing mercy. Finding the enemy in his power the king would have smitten them. Elisha, using the power of God, dare not neglect the mercy of God; and this mercy is as great as the power. If the power of God secures a complete victory over "a great host", the mercy of God will provide for the defeated foe "great provision". Again, we say, such are the ways of grace of a great God.

16. The Siege of Samaria
2 Kings 6:24-7:20

The record of the mercy shewn to the Syrian raiders closes with the statement, "So the bands of Syria came no more into the land of Israel." Nevertheless, the hostility of the Syrians to God's people remained. Thus we read, "It came to pass, after this, that Ben-hadad the king of Syria gathered all his host, and went up, and besieged Samaria"—the very city where such signal mercy had been displayed.

The siege makes manifest the depths of evil to which the nation had sunk, and further displays the height to which the grace of God can rise through this, the last public service of Elisha.

Jehoram, the apostate king, was already beholden to Elisha for having saved his life, and rescued his army from destruction. Apparently this great mercy had affected no change either in the king or nation. Now, in the government of God the enemy is allowed to besiege Samaria, leading to "a great famine" in the city. In the fearful straits to which the inhabitants are reduced, the solemn prophecy uttered more than five hundred years before, is fulfilled. Moses had warned the people of God, that if they departed from God, the time would come when, besieged by their enemies, they would be reduced to such straits, that tender and delicate women would secretly eat their young children (Leviticus 26:21-29; Deuteronomy 28:49-57). This abomination had at last come to pass.

This terrible act instead of turning the king to God, becomes the occasion of revealing the enmity of his heart. Hearing of this horror the king rent his clothes in agony, disclosing that "he had sackcloth within upon his flesh". Thus, combined with his evil ways, there was a profession of religion. Alas! men in their distress may, like Jehoram, turn to some religious device, but they do not turn to God. Thus, the king, in spite of the sackcloth on his flesh, vents his rage against God upon the person of the man of God. He says, "God do so and more also to me, if the head of Elisha the son of Shaphat shall stand on him this day." In the presence of this fresh trouble all past mercies are forgotten, and the desperate king threatens the life of the man of God. He lays the blame on the head which alone was free from the sin. Thereupon he sends a messenger to Elisha's house, where the elders were assembled in the presence of the prophet.

Elisha, apparently forewarned by God, says, "This son of a murderer hath sent to take away my head." He tells them to shut the door upon the king's messenger, for the sound of his master's feet is behind him. Arrived at the door the king dares to say, "Behold this evil is of the Lord; what should I wait for the Lord any longer?"

The awful condition of the nation and the wickedness of the king are thus thoroughly exposed. The people of Samaria are struggling to obtain an ass's head, or a piece of dove's dung. Women are eating their children; the king is raging up and down on the wall; but Elisha is sitting quietly in his house waiting upon the Lord. Then comes the messenger followed by the king charging the Lord with all the evil. The king says as it were, "What is the good of Elisha sitting in his house doing nothing? He delivered me once before from destruction, why does he not act now? What is the good of his professing to wait upon the Lord? Nothing happens. I will give up all thought of the Lord, and I will take off the head of Elisha the prophet of the Lord."

This son of a murderer, who himself has just sworn that he will commit murder, charges the Lord with being the author of all the evil that has come upon the guilty city. Thus the guilt of the nation, in the person of their king, has risen to its height.

Does not this solemn scene foreshadow the yet greater solemnities of the Cross, where the evil of the world rose to its height in condemning the One who, alone of the whole human race, was free of all condemnation? If, however, in the siege of Samaria the sin of the nation is allowed to reveal itself in all its horror, it is that the grace of God may be displayed in all its fulness. Where sin abounds grace does much more abound, thus again foreshadowing that supreme display of grace which, rising above all man's sin at the Cross, takes occasion by that Cross, to proclaim forgiveness and blessing to all the world.

Thus it comes to pass—when the king has thoroughly exposed himself—Elisha, who hitherto had "sat in his house", keeps silence no longer. God's due time had come, for we read, "*Then Elisha said,* Hear ye the word of the Lord." We have heard that what man says exposes the sin of his heart: we are now to hear what God says reveals the grace of His heart. So we read, "Thus saith the Lord, Tomorrow about this time shall a measure of fine flour be sold for a shekel, and two measures of barley for a shekel, in the gate of Samaria."

THE SIEGE OF SAMARIA

In this message of grace there is not a word said about the abominations that had taken place in the city—not a word about the daring wickedness of the king. There is only the unconditional announcement of blessing, in pure sovereign grace, to the very city in which sin had risen to its height; for all this blessing would be seen *"in the gate of Samaria"*.

So again we are reminded of that far greater announcement of grace that sends a message of repentance and forgiveness, to be preached in the name of Christ among all nations; but that message is to begin *"at Jerusalem"*. It is to all nations, for all are guilty, but it begins at the blackest spot in all the world. There is no word of the awful guilt of the city, no word of the daring and blasphemous enmity of the leaders, but, in sovereign unconditional grace, forgiveness is proclaimed in the Name of Jesus to the very city that nailed Him to the Cross.

> *"The very spear that pierced His side*
> *Drew forth the blood to save."*

Thus the ruin of the nation has been made manifest, and the grace of God announced. We are now to see how man treats God's grace. First, the nobleman, on whose arm the king leaned, treats the message with mocking unbelief, only to hear his doom. "Thou shalt see it with thine eyes, but thou shalt not eat thereof." Not many of the rich and great of this world are called.

Then there come before us, four leprous men—convicted sinners as we should say. They realize, what the nobleman did not, that it is either certain death, *or* the grace of God. The Syrian host is before them, a famishing city behind them, and death surrounds them. They rise up and face death, to find that if their desperate need has driven them into the place of death, it has driven them into a place where the Lord has gained a mighty victory. They find the Lord had been before them; "The Lord had made the host of the Syrians to hear a noise of chariots, and a noise of horses, even the noise of a great host." The chariots and horses that had waited upon Elijah at his translation, that had surrounded Elisha for his preservation, are now dealing with the enemies of the Lord in righteous judgment. If grace is to be shewn to guilty sinners, the enemy must first be met and vanquished in righteous judgment.

If, however, the enemy is to be vanquished, it must be the work of the Lord. No one was with the Lord when He annulled the power of the enemy. The city is in desperate need, and can do nothing. The Lord does all the work; and the city, in sovereign grace, partakes of the blessing. There was no man with the Lord of glory when He went to the Cross. Alone He anticipated the terror of Calvary; alone He met the enemy; alone He suffered on the Cross; alone He endured the forsaking; alone He bore the judgment. But guilty sinners, who believe, share in the spoils of His victory. And this we see in picture, for the lepers "did eat and drink" and find silver and gold and raiment.

Further, they spread the "good tidings". They say, "If we hold our peace … some mischief will come upon us." The selfishness of our nature would keep quiet, thus bringing mischief upon ourselves. It may be that we have so feebly tasted of the grace of God, and so little apprehended how greatly we have been enriched with silver and gold and raiment of divine providing, that we have little to say, and hence remain silent, with the result we are in danger of slipping back into the world, and some mischief coming upon us. It is well when, like the blind man of the Gospel, we confess the little we do know, so that we not only retain what we have, but increase our light and blessing.

These four men make a bold confession. They commence with the porter of the city—a very humble man. He tells the porters of the king's house, and they, in turn, tell the good news to the king's house within; and at last it reaches the king's ears. Thus the good news spread from the lowest to the highest in the land.

The king is a very different character from the lepers, and represents a different state of soul. He is not indifferent, for he arose in the night. Still less is he a rejector of the good news, like the nobleman; but he is not a simple believer like the four leprous men. He does not in bold unbelief refuse the good tidings, but he reasons about them. Faith is a matter of the conscience and the heart, not a matter of reasoning. The word runs, "If thou shalt believe in thine heart". Some like the lepers readily believe in the heart, others like the king are slow of heart to believe. Behind the slowness of heart is a reasoning mind and a lack of sense of need. The reasoning mind of the king says, "I will shew you what the Syrians have done." However, as in the case of Naaman there were some wise servants who pleaded with him, so now there is a wise servant ready to meet the king's reasonings. He will put them to the test by sending out two witnesses. In result they trace the evidences of the enemy "unto Jordan". We can trace all our enemies to the Cross, there to see them no more. In the death of Christ every enemy was dealt with for the believer.

So the messengers return, and the slow-hearted king enters into the blessing as much as the whole-hearted lepers, and the starving people of the city. The only man who missed the blessing is the infidel scoffer—the lord on whose arm the king leaned. In the crush at the gate of the city he was trodden upon and died. It might appear as an unfortunate accident, but the government of God was behind it, and the word of the prophet was fulfilled, "Behold, thou shalt see it with thine eyes, but thou shalt not eat thereof." Nor is it otherwise in our day for those who reject the grace of God. For such the word says, "Behold, ye despisers, and wonder, and perish."

17. The Seven Years' Famine
2 KINGS 8:1-6

The siege of Samaria with all its horrors, and the grace of God in all its fulness, were soon forgotten. Neither misery endured, nor mercy received, turned the nation to the Lord their God. Nevertheless, God does not abandon His people. He still acts on their behalf, even though it may be in the way of chastening because of their evil. Thus we find Elisha saying, "The Lord hath called for a famine." It is not only revealed to the prophet that a famine is coming, but, that it is sent directly by the Lord, proving the truth of that word which says, "Surely the Lord God will do nothing, but He revealeth His secret unto His servants the prophets."

Further, it is revealed to Elisha that if God chastens His people, He also sets a limit to the trial. The famine in Israel shall come upon the land for seven years. Nor is it otherwise in the history of the Church, and of individuals, in this present day. Of the Church in Smyrna we read, "Ye shall have tribulation", but it is limited to "ten days". So, too, if there is a needs be for God's people, individually, to pass through manifold trials, they will last but "for a season" (1 Peter 1:6).

Moreover, we learn that if the Lord calls for a famine because of the low condition of the nation, He will also provide for the godly during the time of famine. Thus, once more, we see the grace of God to the Shunammite. This godly woman, who had cared for the prophet in days of prosperity, is now warned and instructed by the prophet in days of adversity. Her circumstances apparently have changed. It would seem she is now a widow with her only son. She is told to leave the land during the years of famine.

At the end of the seven years she returns to the Land and appeals to the king for the restoration of her house and land. The king is talking with Gehazi, who is identified as the servant of the man of God. His circumstances also appear to have changed. Years ago he had coveted "oliveyards and vineyards, sheep, oxen, menservants and maidservants", and now, by means of his possessions, he has climbed the social ladder until he has become the associate and companion of royalty. The king would fain beguile an hour by hearing of the "great things" that Elisha had done. Gehazi is in company with the great men of the world, but if he would speak of "great things" he must needs go back in thought to other days when he companied with the lowly man of God. The "great things" that Elisha did are only a recollection with Gehazi.

It may, however, be that there was a work of grace in the heart of Gehazi leading his thoughts from the earthly riches he had gained, to the spiritual blessings he had lost. Be this as it may, he certainly becomes a witness before the king of the grace of God as seen in the "great things that Elisha had done". Moreover, the Lord uses Gehazi to restore house and lands to the Shunammite, as before He had used Elisha in warning her to leave them. But how different the way in which these men are used. Elisha is used as one who is in the intimacy of a friend with the Lord, enjoying the confidences of the Lord. Gehazi is used as the friend and intimate of a wicked king. Elisha speaks as one who is intelligent in the mind of the Lord. Gehazi speaks as circumstances and coincidences dictate. For, as he is recounting his reminiscences in the service of Elisha, behold, the woman and her son, who had part in the greatest of the "great things", appears before the king. This apparently strange coincidence is used by the Lord to restore the Shunammite's possessions.

Nor will it be otherwise with the God-fearing remnant of Israel, in a day yet to come, of whom possibly the widowed Shunammite is a figure. Like this woman who had known the grace of God, the godly remnant, on the ground of grace, will be brought back to the inheritance of their Land, and receive, in the excess of blessing, all that they have lost during the time of exile from the Land of their fathers.

It is happy thus to trace the hand of the Lord using men—whether prophets, servants, or kings—and behind every circumstance and coincidence, making all things work together for good to them that love Him.

18. The King of Syria

2 KINGS 8:7-15

Elisha's service is not confined to Israel and the Land. Thus we read he "came to Damascus", and is found amongst the Gentiles. Ben-hadad, the king of Syria, is sick. In his sickness he recognises and honours the man of God. In his prosperity the king had sent a great host to capture him: in his sickness he sends a great gift to honour him. In health he seeks to encompass him for his destruction: in sickness he seeks to propitiate him for his assistance. Driven by need he recognises and owns the God that hitherto he had despised. Such is man, and such our hearts. The world, when faced with some dire calamity, will, in an outward way, recognise and turn to God. Alas! even the believer may walk carelessly, with little reference to God, when all things run smoothly, and circumstances are prosperous, and health is good. But in our troubles we have to turn to God, and well it is that we do turn to God and have such a God of grace to turn to; though far better, like Enoch of old, to walk with God, and thus, like the Apostle be able to say, "I have learned, in whatsoever state I am, therewith to be content. I know both how to be abased, and I know how to abound: everywhere and in all things I am instructed both to be full and to be hungry, both to abound and to suffer need."

Elisha was evidently one who, in his day, walked with the Lord, and received communications from the Lord. Thus he can say, in answer to the messenger, "Thou mayest certainly recover." There was nothing fatal in the disease. Howbeit, the prophet adds, "The Lord hath shewed me that he shall surely die." Thus Elisha intimates that Benhadad is going to die, though by other means than the sickness.

As he delivers this message the prophet is visibly affected. Foreseeing all the misery that is coming upon the people of God, he weeps. Hazael, contemplating the murder of his master, feels uneasy in the presence of the man of God. His conscience makes him ashamed. He enquires, "Why weepeth my lord?" Elisha's answer clearly shows that he is not moved to tears by the illness of the king, or the wickedness of Hazael, but on account of the suffering that God's people will endure at the hands of Hazael. Elisha closes his public ministry by weeping over a people who were unmoved by all his miracles of grace. Thus he foreshadows his far greater Master who, in the closing days of His ministry of grace, wept over the city that had rejected His grace and spurned His love. One, too, who could say to the women of Jerusalem, "Weep not for Me, but weep for yourselves, and for your children. For, behold, the days are coming, in the which they shall say, Blessed are the barren, and the wombs that never bare, and the paps which never gave suck."

In like spirit, Elisha, knowing the future career of Hazael, foretells the depths of evil and cruelty to which he will sink. "I know", says the prophet, "the evil thou wilt do unto the children of Israel: their strongholds wilt thou set on fire, and their young men wilt thou slay with the sword, and wilt dash their children, and rip up their women with child."

Hazael protests that he is not a dog that he should act with such callous brutality. Probably his protest is entirely sincere. Such deeds might have been foreign to his thoughts, and even abhorrent to his feelings, at the moment. He did not know his own heart. He was not aware that the heart is deceitful above all things, and desperately wicked. As with ourselves, too often, he little realized the depth of wickedness and cruelty in the heart that is held in check by many a safeguard until, suddenly aroused by circumstances which give the occasion, it blazes forth in all its horror. Instead of asking, "Is thy servant a dog?" far better would it have been for Hazael, as for ourselves, to take the ground of the Syrophenician woman who owned that she was indeed a dog, only to discover that there is grace in the heart of God even for a dog (Mark 7:24-30).

In Hazael's history the immediate circumstances were ripe to manifest the wickedness of his heart. Thus Elisha simply answers, "The Lord hath shewed me that thou shalt be king over Syria." Without further word, Hazael "departed from Elisha, and came to his master". He acts the hypocrite before the king, giving part of Elisha's message, but keeping back the fact that he would surely die. The opportunity has come for this murderer. As prime minister he has access to the king, and the illness offered a favourable opportunity to an unscrupulous man to usurp the throne. The idea of wielding great power, as the reigning monarch, had such irresistible attraction to Hazael that he is ready to contemplate even murder to gain his end. The sickness and weakness of the king made murder appear so easy. The sickness would be such a simple way to cover the murder. All would know that the king was ill, and fearing he might not recover had sent a prime minister to the prophet to enquire if he should die. No one need know what Elisha had said to Hazael. What more easy than to take a thick damp cloth and suffocate the helpless king, already weakened by sickness, and then give out to the world that the sickness had terminated fatally.

So it came to pass; the prime minister becomes a murderer, and the murderer a usurper of the throne. The man that reaches a throne by murder will not hesitate to seek to maintain that throne by violence and cruelty. As Elisha foresees Hazael will carry the fire and the sword among the people of God.

19. The Anointing of Jehu
2 Kings 9

The mighty miracles of Elisha—the witnesses of the grace of God to a guilty nation—have all been in vain. Israel refuses to turn from idols to the living God. The prophet may weep over the sorrows coming upon the nation, may foretell their miseries, be used to appoint the instruments that will be used to execute judgment, but, though he lives to a ripe old age, we hear of miracles no more.

Thus it comes to pass that Elisha sends one of the children of the prophets to anoint Jehu to be king, by the word of the Lord. The young man is to carry out his commission in a way that will clearly show Elisha has nothing in common with Jehu; for, having delivered his message, he is to "open the door, and flee, and tarry not."

The young man had two announcements to make to Jehu; first, that the Lord had anointed him to be "king over the people of the Lord, even over Israel." Second, he was to smite the house of Ahab, and thus avenge the blood of the servants, and prophets, of the Lord, shed by the wicked Jezebel.

THE ANOINTING OF JEHU

To reach the throne was entirely in accord with the ambitions of Jehu. To smite the house of Ahab would appear to Jehu a sound policy to establish himself as king. Hence he carries out the directions of the Lord with the greatest possible energy and zeal. However, God's motives were not Jehu's. God was dealing with evil, avenging the blood of his servants, and maintaining His own glory. Jehu was getting rid of all those who could oppose his ambitions. Jehu is very zealous in dealing with evil when it suits his own purpose, but quite indifferent to evil when he concludes it is politic to leave it alone. So it comes to pass he ruthlessly avenges the sins of the house of Ahab, while leaving untouched the sins of the house of Jeroboam. He destroys the worship of Baal; he preserves the golden calves. His hand was ready to use the sword against the enemies of the Lord, when it suited his own ends; his heart was utterly indifferent to the law of the Lord. So we read, "Jehu took no heed to walk in the law of the Lord God of Israel with all his heart" (2 Kings 10:28-31).

God, in His righteous judgment, while using Jehu to deal with the wicked house of Ahab is not unmindful of the mixed motives that energised Jehu, and the fact that in carrying out the vengeance of the Lord, he was simply indulging his own cruel heart for his own ends. If God has to deal in judgment, it is His strange work. If Jehu undertakes to deal with evil, it is to him a congenial task. Hence it is that while God uses Jehu to execute judgment on Jezreel, yet He says, by the prophet Hosea, "I will avenge the blood of Jezreel upon the house of Jehu; and will cause to cease the kingdom of the house of Israel" (Hosea 1:4).

20. The Death of Elisha
2 Kings 13:14-25

Elisha, at the direction of the Lord, had sent a young man to anoint Jehu as king. The young man having carried out his errand was instructed to flee, and not tarry with Jehu. The prophet thus clearly showing that between himself and this violent and unprincipled man there was nothing in common. Jehu, on his side, while willing to carry out instructions that accord with his ambitions, had no regard for the man of God. Thus during his reign, and that of his son, the prophet is entirely ignored. For a period of forty-five years we hear nothing of Elisha.

During these years the kings and the people depart from the Lord and pursue an evil course. Jehu took no heed to walk in the law of the Lord, the sins of Jeroboam are not departed from. His son, Jehoahaz, did that which was evil in the sight of the Lord. In consequence the anger of the Lord was kindled against Israel, and they are delivered into the hands of their enemies (2 Kings 10:31-33; 13:1-3).

In the reign of Joash, the succeeding king, the long life of Elisha came to its close. Joash, wicked man though he was, could appreciate godliness in others. Doubtless he felt that the presence of Elisha in the land was a real power for good.

THE DEATH OF ELISHA

Therefore, he was genuinely troubled at the approach of the prophet's death. The king weeps at the death bed of Elisha, and appears to realize that the chariots of Israel and the horsemen thereof, that had rapt Elijah to heaven, were now waiting upon Elisha in his closing moments.

Joash, like his father and grandfather, had neglected the prophet in his life; and yet, when at length he visits him, he finds, even in the prophet's dying moments, that Elisha is strong in the delivering grace of the Lord. The king is told to take bow and arrows; to put his hand on the bow. Then Elisha put his hand on the king's hand, whereupon the king is bidden to shoot. Elisha interprets the act as symbolizing that the king's hand, strengthened by the hand of the representative of the Lord, would bring deliverance from his enemies.

Is not the king thus reminded of how much he had lost by his neglect of the man of God? Had he but turned to the prophet before, would he not have found the power and mercy of God with him to deliver him from all his enemies? Has the king even yet learnt his lesson? Elisha will put him to the test. The prophet seems to say, "I have shewn you the significance of this arrow—that it means a victory over your enemies now take arrows and smite upon the ground."

Alas! The faith of the king falls short of the resources of God. The king smote thrice and stayed. Had his faith been more simple would he not have emptied his quiver of arrows? There was power at his disposal to effect complete deliverance from the enemy; there was neither faith nor spiritual discernment to use it. How often, like the king, we are brought into circumstances in which only faith and spirituality will know how to act. Alas! Too often such circumstances discover our low condition.

The king is rebuked for his lack of faith; though he is told that the mercy of the Lord will be exercised three times on his behalf. Thus the last utterance of this honoured servant of the Lord foretells the delivering mercy of the Lord, and is in keeping with the ministry of the grace of God that had characterised his long life.

It would seem by the allusion to "the chariot of Israel, and the horsemen thereof" that king Joash anticipated that Elisha would be rapt to heaven after the pattern of Elijah. When, however, we come to the actual account of his end, there is no outward display of supernatural power. In striking contrast to the close of Elijah's path, we have only the simple record, "Elisha died, and they buried him."

None the less, God will honour his devoted servant in His own way and time. God put great honour upon Moses by giving him a private burial. Perhaps, however, the greatest honour is reserved for Elisha: for, in keeping with his ministry of grace, God uses his death to illustrate the greatest of all the wonders of grace, the bringing life out of death. Thus, at the coming in of the year a dead man is buried in the sepulchre of Elisha, and, we read, touching the bones of Elisha, "he revived and stood upon his feet".

"When thou shalt make his soul an offering for sin, he shall see a seed", is written of the One of whom Elisha was only a type. When the Lord Jesus goes into death, He secures a seed. "Except the grain of wheat fall into the ground and die, it abideth alone: but if it die, it bringeth forth much fruit." Is not this great mystery foreshadowed in this fine scene? The enemy held the people of God in bondage, death was upon them, and all man could do was to bury his dead. But when death comes in contact with one who typically had gone into death in grace—one who, as we might say, had refused to pass to glory by the chariot of horsemen, and had chosen the way of the grave—there is, as the glorious result, life and resurrection. The man revived and stood upon his feet. And, further, if there is life from the dead, there is also deliverance from the enemy; for we read, The Lord was gracious unto His people and "had compassion on them, and had respect unto them, because of His covenant with Abraham, Isaac, and Jacob, and would not destroy them neither cast He them from His presence".

Thus closes the marvellous history of this man of God, whose high privilege it was to be an exponent of the grace of God in the midst of an apostate nation, and before an evil world.

Like a heavenly stranger he passes on his way morally apart from all, while in grace the servant of all, accessible alike to rich and poor. He is found in every condition of life; he comes into contact with every class of men; he moves at times within the land of Israel, and at times he passes beyond its bounds. But, wherever he is, in whatsoever circumstances he is found, with whomsoever he comes in contact, his one unvarying business is to make known the grace of God.

At times he is mocked; at times he is ignored and forgotten; at times men plot to take his life; but in spite of all opposition he pursues his service of love, removing the curse, preserving the lives of kings, feeding the hungry, helping the needy, healing the leper and raising the dead.

He allows nothing in his ways and manner of life that is inconsistent with his ministry of grace. He refuses the riches of this world, and the gifts of men, content himself to be poor that others may be enriched.

Thus he becomes a fitting type of that far greater One by whom grace and truth came into this world; who dwelt among us full of grace and truth; who became poor that we might be rich; who endured the contradiction of sinners, and who, at last gave up His life that grace might reign through righteousness.

Further, if Elisha is a type of the Christ who was to come, he is also the pattern for every believer in Christ, teaching us that, amidst all the circumstances of life, we should be the exponents, in a needy world, of the grace that has reached us in all our degradation in order to have us at last with, and like, the Man in the glory, where for ever we shall be to the praise of the glory of His grace.

OTHER BOOKS BY HAMILTON SMITH

"THE LORD IS MY SHEPHERD" AND OTHER PAPERS
    ISBN 978-0-901860-06-4; Scripture Truth Publications
    97 pages; Paperback; July 1987

THE GOSPEL OF MARK: AN EXPOSITORY OUTLINE
    144 pages; March 2007; Scripture Truth Publications
    ISBN 978-0-901860-69-9 (Paperback)
    ISBN 978-0-901860-70-5 (Hardback)

ELIJAH: A PROPHET OF THE LORD
    ISBN 978-0-901860-68-2; Scripture Truth Publications
    80 pages; Paperback; March 2007

www.ingramcontent.com/pod-product-compliance
Lightning Source LLC
Chambersburg PA
CBHW032207040426
42449CB00005B/469